Practical Woodwork

'WOODWORK IS A MOST SATISFYING CRAFT'

PRACTICAL WOODWORK

CHARLES H. HAYWARD

Editor of WOODWORKER
Author of Cabinet making for Beginners
Practical Veneering, Tools for Woodwork
Light Machines for Woodwork, etc.

DRAKE PUBLISHERS INC.
NEW YORK · LONDON

Published in 1978 by
Drake Publishers, Inc.
801 Second Ave.
New York, N.Y. 10017

Copyright Ⓒ 1965 by Evans Brothers Limited
All rights reserved

Library of Congress Cataloging in Publication Data

Hayward, Charles Harold, 1898-
   Practical woodwork.

   (Drake home craftsman series)
   Reprint of the 1967 ed. published by Emerson
Books, New York.
   Includes index.
   1. Woodwork.   I. Title
TT180.H3884   1978   684'.08   77-18405
ISBN 0-8473-1683-1

Printed in the United States of America

Introduction

THERE HAVE BEEN many developments in woodwork over the last few years, developments in both materials, adhesives, finishes, and power tools. It is true that hand woodwork has not changed basically but anyone doing woodwork for the first time today has both advantages and limitations compared with the conditions of a few years ago.

On the credit side there is the availability of reliable plywood, blockboard, chipboard, plastic sheets, and so on; in adhesives there is a wide range of special quality cements; modern finishes include the many heat- and liquid-resisting polishes; and the development of small power tools enables many operations to be performed that would be extremely difficult or laborious by purely hand methods.

As against this there is the disappearance of many of the solid timbers, especially those in the smaller thicknesses.

In this book the author has presented the modern approach to woodwork, giving the basic essentials of the craft for the man who prefers hand methods, and at the same time explaining how light power tools can be used to advantage for some operations.

Woodwork is a most satisfying craft, which not only enables many attractive things to be made, but which is intensely interesting in itself. Its simplest requirements are within the range of everyone, and its more advanced work presents a challenge to anyone with the desire to make things. The proof of this lies in the fact that the man who once takes it up invariably retains his interest in it for the rest of his life.

Contents

1 Tools

THERE ARE CERTAIN basic tools a man must have to do woodwork, their range depending largely upon the type of work he does. Right at the outset we advise him to obtain them, and to add to them as the need for others becomes obvious. For a start a large kit is not needed, but it is a mistake to handicap oneself by lack of essential tools. Furthermore, they should be good ones, because it is not long before the limitations of poor ones become obvious. If so-called cheap tools are obtained (in reality they are not cheap) a man can always blame the tools when things do not turn out as hoped, and possibly with good reason. If he obtains tools of a reputable make he at least avoids this temptation.

Possibilities of Machines
For a start the range of tools needed is not great, but it is as well to have an eye to the future, and this brings us straightway to the question of power. Today it is seldom that a man does all his work by hand. There is surely no virtue in hard slogging work merely as such. There are in fact many operations which a machine will do not only far more quickly and easily than a man can do by hand, but it will also do them better.

As a simple example assume that a number of rails and stiles is required. A circular saw will cut them straighter and to far closer limits than one could saw by hand. Furthermore, they will be perfectly square and need little more than a skim with the plane. It is as well, therefore, to consider the advantages of such a machine and its possible installation at a later date—if indeed one has the facilities for it.

At the outset, however, we should like to stress the importance of safety precautions. Any powered machine is potentially dangerous in inexperienced hands, even the smallest, but if properly used and the obvious safety measures taken, there is little danger. This assumes, of course, that the machine itself is of a good make and designed to give full protection.

Machine Saws
As the installation of one or more machines necessarily affects the range of hand-tools required we have given alternative kits, these depending upon which

machine is chosen. To an extent the choice is affected by the type of work one does, but generally speaking the most useful all-round machine is the circular saw because, in addition to ripping, cross-cutting, mitring, and so on, it will work grooves and rebates and cut tenons. If with tilting-table or tilting-saw it will also angle-cut, and if so equipped will work mouldings. This covers a wide range of operations needed in general woodwork and is thus an obvious first choice. It will not cut curves, however, and if one's work entails much of this the band-saw is invaluable. It is the fastest-cutting saw for external curves, and can also be used for straight cutting, though it is not so efficient for this as the circular saw. Tenons and angle halvings can be cut but it will neither groove nor rebate. If internal curves have to be cut the jig-saw is essential, though it is much slower cutting than the band-saw.

Planer

For a rather different series of operations there is the planer which will surface or edge within the limits of its table width. This is a time-saving machine because, apart from planing quickly, it eliminates the necessity for testing the work for squareness (assuming that it is properly used). For thicknessing timber, however, either a thicknessing machine is needed or a thicknessing attachment. The latter is the more usual in the small workshop.

Rebating up to the cutter width, and in depth up to the clearance above the main bearing, can be done if the machine is provided with a rebating table. It should be mentioned that for cabinet work or joinery it is necessary to skim by hand afterwards to remove the inevitable planer marks.

Sander

So far as the small workshop is concerned the rigid disc sander is the most generally used, though its purpose is that of trimming rather than of smoothing. It will be realized that the necessarily circular path of the abrasive granules makes it unsuitable for work to have a polished finish. However, for trimming mitres or square butt joints, it is excellent. The belt sander, in which the abrasive runs in a straight line, can be used for smoothing small parts, and when the drum at one end is exposed this can be used for hollow shapes.

Mortiser

This is useful to those who do much framing work. The two most generally used types are the hollow chisel and the rotary miller. The former cuts square ended mortises in a series of stabs. The rotary miller machine in its nature will only cut mortises with rounded ends, these having to be finished square afterwards by hand. On the other hand, it is quick cutting and can also be used for grooving and sometimes for rebating.

Combination Machine

The space taken up by individual machines is often more than can be afforded in the small workshop, and as a result various combinations of universal machines have been designed. Where space is available it is invariably better to have separate machines, because clearly a machine which is designed for a single purpose will do that job better than one which has to compromise between several. This is apart from the time taken in having to remove one attachment to enable another to be set up. On the other hand, for the small workshop, the machine capable of doing several jobs has its advantages.

The chief types of machines are: the universal machine, the basic lathe with attachments, and the radial-arm saw. Of these the first is generally used more in the trade, and in accordance with the type will do various operations. These are generally: circular sawing and boring, and planing and sanding.

Occasionally a mortising device is fitted. As a rule the saw is of larger size with more powerful motor than in the other machines.

Basic Lathe

This has many advantages, and with its attachments will do many operations. These attachments include circular saw, band-saw, jig-saw (in some models), planer (thicknessing attachment also available), disc and belt sanders, drilling head, mortiser, flexible drive, etc. In some machines the circular saw and planer can remain permanently in position.

Radial-arm Saw

The radial-arm saw works on a different principle from the others. The saw is directly attached to the motor, and the whole travels along an arm which may allow movement of some 24 in., and which is free to be pivoted around its supporting column at any angle. The arm can be raised or lowered, and the carriage which holds the motor can be pivoted both horizontally and vertically. It is thus clear that an extremely wide range of movements is possible. Furthermore, since the tool is always above the wood, it is always possible to see exactly what it is doing. The attachments, apart from the circular saw, include: router, drilling head, jig-saw, disc sander, and lathe.

Powered Hand-tools

Apart from fixed floor or bench machines there is a range of powered hand-tools. Of these the circular saw is the most useful for general woodwork, though those whose work involves much shape cutting will prefer the jig-saw. The latter is, of course, much slower cutting than the circular saw. Sanders of either the belt or orbital type can save a lot of laborious work.

So far as the electric drill is concerned its use in woodwork is generally

9

confined to drilling screw holes, etc., though many makes have various attachments which can be used with them. Their limited power, however, has to be realized. They are suitable for light work only, and the man who has much use for such a tool would be better advised to obtain the individual portable machine—saw, sander, etc.

Router
Of these individual powered hand-tools the router is rather a special case. It is a high-speed machine capable of many operations. Among the jobs it will do are grooving, rebating, moulding, and recessing, and it will work equally well around a curve as along the straight. Furthermore, its high speed enables it to work against the grain with a minimum of tearing out, often without tearing out at all. Another point about it is that it can be turned upside down and fixed beneath a bench, in which form it virtually becomes a small spindle moulder or shaper. It is somewhat expensive, but for the man who is able to make use of it is not only a time-saving tool, but one which will do jobs which would be extremely difficult or impossible to do by other methods.

Hand-tools
It does not follow that because a certain machine is installed that all comparable hand-tools are unnecessary. For instance, it is often more convenient to use a hand-saw to cross-cut a board than to use a machine—in fact, it may be the only way. Similarly, wood for cabinet work still needs to be hand-planed although it may have been passed through a surface planer or thicknesser. In the following we have, therefore, given a list of basic hand-tools and have noted those which could be eliminated on the assumption that various machines are installed.

Hand-saw, cross-cut 24 in., about 9 points per inch.

Back-saw, 10 in., about 14 points per inch.

Bow-saw.

Jack plane, metal adjustable, 14 in., 2 in., cutter; or wood plane, 2 in. cutter.

Smoothing plane, metal adjustable, 9 in., 2 in., cutter.

Rebate and fillister plane, metal adjustable.

Grooving plane (plough), preferably with range of 8 or more cutters. Less expensive alternative with 3 cutters only.

Chisels, $1\frac{1}{4}$ in. bevel-edged.

$\quad\quad\frac{1}{2}$ in. firmer.

$\quad\quad\frac{1}{4}$ in. firmer.

$\quad\quad\frac{5}{16}$ in. sash mortise.

Screw-driver, 8 in., cabinet pattern.

$\quad\quad\quad$ 5 in. ratchet.

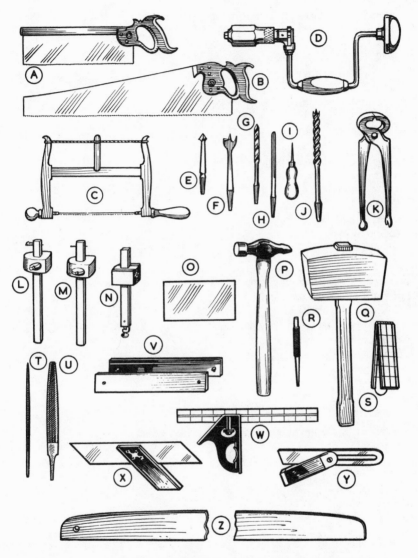

Fig. 1. HAND-TOOLS NEEDED BY THE WOODWORKER
A. Back-saw. B. Hand-saw. C. Bow-saw. D. Ratchet brace. E, F, G, H, J. Bits.
I. Bradawl. K. Pincers. L, M, N. Gauges. O. Scraper. P. Hammer. Q. Mallet.
R. Punch. S. Rule. T, U. Files. V. Parallel strips. W. Square. X. Mitre square.
Y. Sliding bevel. Z. Straight-edge

Hammer, 8 oz. Warrington or London pattern.
Mallet, 6 in.
Pincers, 8 in.
Brace, 8 in. sweep, ratchet.
Bits, $\frac{3}{8}$ in. twist; shell, about $\frac{1}{8}$ in., or half-twist for screws; $\frac{3}{4}$ in. or 1 in. centre; snail counter-sink.
Bradawl, for usual screw sizes.
Oilstone, 8 in. by 2 in., fine grade.
Glass-paper rubber, cork, about $4\frac{1}{2}$ in.
Rule, 2 ft. or 3 ft. folding.
Try-square, 12 in. adjustable.
Cutting gauge.
Marking gauge.
Mortise gauge.
Scraper, 5 in.
Punch, hollow point.

The following tools need not be obtained straightway, but can be bought as the need for them is felt.
Spokeshave, wood, about $2\frac{1}{4}$ in. blade, or metal, round face.
Half-round rasp, about 7 in.
Half-round file, about 7 in.
Keyhole-saw.
Sash cramps, pair, 3 ft.
G cramps, pair, 9 in.
Mitre square.
Sliding bevel.
Bullnose plane.
Metal router.

Early on the following appliances should be made.
Bench hook.
Shooting board, 3–4 ft.
Straight-edge 3–4 ft.
Pair parallel strips.
Mitre block.
Mitre box.
Mitre shooting board.

If a circular saw is installed the need for the plough or grooving plane largely disappears. The rebate plane may still be desirable, however, to enable rebates to be smoothed. A band-saw largely removes the need for bow-saw and keyhole-saw, but they may be required for internal cuts, and for small special work. The jig-saw will replace the bow-saw entirely. An electric

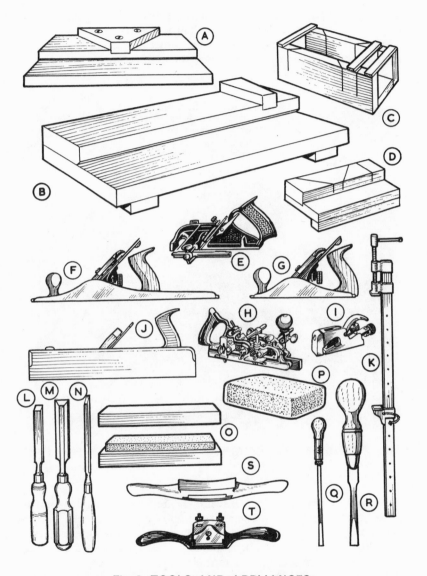

Fig. 2. TOOLS AND APPLIANCES
A, B. Shooting boards. C. Mitre box. D. Mitre block. E, F, G, H, I, J. Planes.
K. Sash cramp. L, M, N. Chisels. O. Oilstone. P. Glasspaper rubber. Q, R.
Screwdrivers. S, T. Spokeshaves

drill, assuming that there are small morse drills, will make small bits unnecessary, but larger bits are still needed for the brace; also the countersink.

Taken all round it will be realized, then, that for the small workshop the installation of machines does not remove the need for many hand-tools.

Fig. 3. TENONING ON CIRCULAR SAW USING PUSHER STICK

The writer's advice to the man who is going in for general woodwork—making furniture and fitments, small items, and garden woodwork is to install either a basic lathe with circular-saw attachment, or a radial-arm saw. In both cases further attachments can be added as the need arises. One advantage of the basic lathe is that a normal pattern planer and thicknesser can be added, whereas with the radial-arm saw this cannot be done.

It is assumed that a bench of some sort is available. A length of 4 ft. 6 in. is the minimum really useful size. It should have a vice and adjustable stop. If space is a difficulty it might be of the collapsible type hinged to the wall.

MAINTENANCE OF TOOLS

All tools, if they are to do their work properly, must be properly sharpened and kept in condition; with machines it is vital because, apart from being inaccurate, they can be ineffective and even dangerous. It is impossible in the limited space of this book to include full details of sharpening and using. The main idea only is attempted. Those seeking fuller information should see *Light Machines for Woodwork* in which the whole thing is discussed fully.

Circular Saw

The saw should project above the table about $\frac{1}{2}$ in. more than the thickness of the wood. The riving knife must be in alignment and the guard fitted. When ripping the fence must be parallel with the saw, and for grooving and

Fig. 4. (A) RADIAL AND (B) BRIAR TEETH

rebating an extension to the fence is necessary so that the wood has a bearing surface throughout the entire cut. Do not let the fingers approach the saw closely, but use a pusher stick as in Fig. 3.

As soon as a saw loses its keenness it should be sharpened straightway. A blunt saw can give rise to all sorts of trouble. That it will cut slowly is the least of these. Worse features are the heat generated by the teeth which rub rather than cut, resulting in the wood being burnt and most likely in a buckled saw brought on by loss of tension and by the saw having to be forced. It is because of this necessity that two blades are desirable so that one can be in use whilst the other is being sharpened.

For the small saw either radial teeth or briar cross-cut teeth are desirable. These are shown in Fig. 4. To sharpen either a special vice is needed, this having a rounded top and centre bolt. The teeth are first set, that is, bent sideways in alternate directions. The professional sharpener uses a hammer and special anvil, and it is probably the most satisfactory way, but the pliers type of set is handy and simpler to use. Do not overdo the set, as it merely means that the saw is removing wood unnecessarily without gain.

The saw is then held in the vice and each alternate 'V' filed, the file thus bearing on the front of one tooth and on the rear of that adjoining. The file is horizontal, and is turned at an angle of about 80 degrees. Finally, the saw is reversed and the remaining teeth sharpened. Many men prefer to have a saw sharpened by a professional sharpener.

Band-saw

This can be sharpened a few times, the saw being held in a long vice and the file taken straight across, every gullet being sharpened.

Planer

The blades of this machine are fixed to the cutter block in various ways, but it is only a matter of withdrawing the bolts and removing the caps or wedges. If the cutters are not too bad they can be brought into condition with the hone only, a special holder being used to grip the cutter at a convenient angle. The bevel is rubbed until a burr can be detected at the back, after which the latter is rubbed flat to turn back the burr. To get rid of the latter finally draw a block of wood along the edge. This sometimes damages the edge, but a rub first on the bevel then on the flat restores it.

Most machines have each cutter independently adjustable, but in some the wedge fixing draws it to the bottom of the slot, and this necessitates the use of the simple appliance shown in Fig. 5, so that the entire edge of every cutter has the same projection at the table. When cutters are too bad to be honed they should be ground, and unless one has the facilities it is advisable to send them to a grinder.

To set the machine, place one cutter in its slot and turn the fixing bolts with finger pressure only. Lower the feeding table out of the way, and adjust the taking-off table so that a straight piece of wood placed on it is just caught by the cutter as it is turned by hand, as in Fig. 6. Test it at both ends so that the cutter has equal projection throughout, and, when satisfactory, tighten the bolts. The remaining cutters are dealt with in the same way, the taking-off table not being moved during the entire operation after the initial positioning. This, in fact, is the normal position for this table in the general run of planing operations.

The feeding table is lower by the required thickness of the chips to be removed. There is, of course, a limit to the amount that can be removed in one pass, especially when the machine is used for hardwood and for surfacing rather than edging. In a small planer the amount taken off in edging would be no more than about $\frac{1}{8}$ in. For surfacing it would be less, and in fact where the purpose is essentially that of truing rather than the rapid reduction of wood it would be little more than a skim.

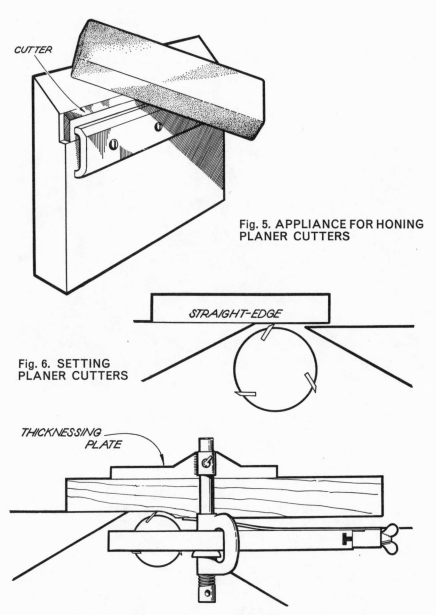

Fig. 5. APPLIANCE FOR HONING PLANER CUTTERS

Fig. 6. SETTING PLANER CUTTERS

Fig. 7. DIAGRAM OF THICKNESSING ATTACHMENT

In use a safety-first measure (apart from the use of the guard) is to avoid having either hand directly over the cutters. At the start of a cut both hands are over the feeding table, and, when a reasonable length has passed beyond the cutters, the left hand is taken over to the taking-off table. Indeed, this should be done as soon as practicable because it is on this table that the truth of the cut is decided. As the end of the wood approaches the cutters both hands bear down on the taking-off table.

Fig. 8. MACHINE PLANER IN USE
Retractable guard is shown drawn back to set reveal cutter

Thicknessing Attachment

This in the main consists of a thicknessing plate supported by a stout column attached to the feeding table. There is, in addition, a flat spring, the purpose of which is to press the wood up against the thicknessing plate. The diagram in Fig. 7 explains the principle of how the device works. In use the one surface of the wood is trued in the ordinary way. It is then passed through with this trued surface uppermost and bearing against the thicknessing plate. The latter is first set so that the thickest part of the wood can clear between it and the spring (the column is usually calibrated to show the clearance), and the feeding table then adjusted till the distance between the thicknessing plate and taking-off table equals the required thickness of the wood.

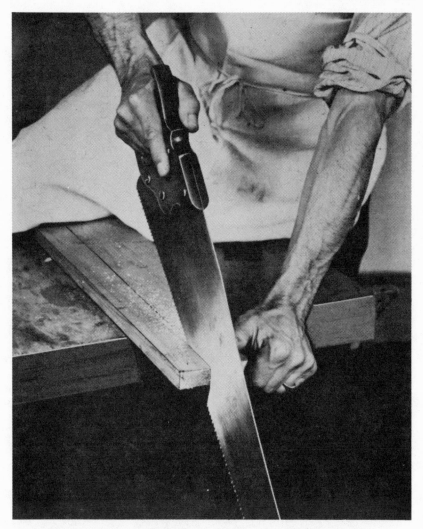

Fig. 9. HOW HAND-SAW IS USED AT START OF CUT

HAND-TOOLS

Hand-saw

For the main cutting up of timber from the board the hand-saw is used. The cross-cut is the most convenient to have because it can be used for cutting both across and with the grain. One of 22 in. length with eight points per inch

19

is a good average size. The index finger should be pointed along the handle as it helps in the control of the saw. When the wood is laid on trestles it can be steadied by pressing down with the knee. Towards the completion of a cross-cut the left hand is brought over to support the overhanging piece, as otherwise the corner is liable to splinter off.

One of the secrets of sawing is to start the cut right, the saw in line with the pencil mark. It is a great help if the handle is held low for the first few strokes as it is easier to judge the alignment. When it has progressed a few inches the normal angle of about 45–50 degrees is used. Get into the habit of

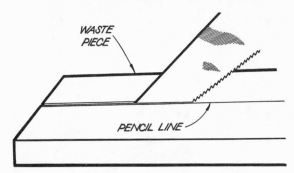

Fig. 10. CUTTING TO WASTE SIDE OF LINE

square cutting as soon as possible. For a start a square can be placed alongside the saw as a guide, but once the correct feel of square sawing has been acquired it should be dispensed with. At the start of the cut hold the thumb of the left hand against the side of the blade as a guide, and move the saw up and down a few short strokes until it has made a start (see Fig. 9). This or a similar position should be retained until the saw has cut in about half the width of its blade, the idea being that if the saw should jump from its kerf the side pressure of thumb or knuckle would prevent it from barking across the hand. Always cut on the waste side of the line, as in Fig. 10, to allow for trimming later with the plane.

Some men prefer the cabinet-maker's overhand rip in which the wood is cramped at the edge of the bench. To start the cut the saw is pointed upwards at an angle in the direction of the line and a few short strokes made. The position in Fig. 11 is then adopted. Many find this method less back-aching.

Back-saw
For general benchwork the back-saw is used, the wood being either held in the vice or supported against the bench hook. The latter is used, as in Fig. 12. Again the thumb of the left hand bears against the side of the blade, particularly at the start of the cut.

To saw a tenon or halving the wood is gripped at an angle in the vice so that its progress along both the end and the side of the tenon can be followed (Fig. 13). The cut is continued until the extent of the diagonal has been sawn, when the wood is reversed in the vice, this time upright, and the cut

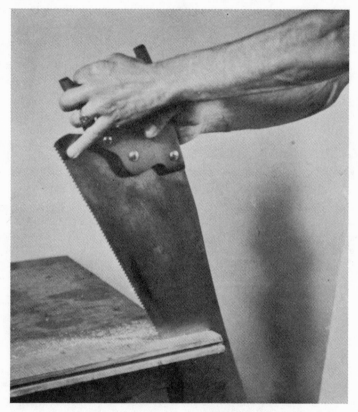

Fig. 11. RIPPING BY OVERHAND METHOD

completed. In all cases hold the saw to the waste side of the line so that the latter is just left in.

When a cut at an angle is needed it is a help to fix the wood in the vice at the angle so that the cut can be upright. An example is in sawing dovetails.

21

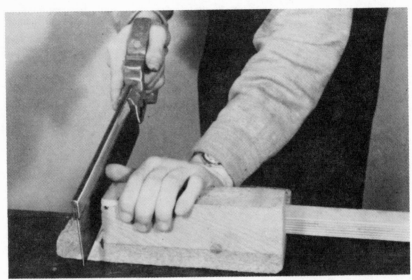

Fig. 12. USING BACK-SAW ON BENCH HOOK

Fig. 13. SAWING TENON IN VICE

At the start of the cut the left thumb bears against the side of the saw, but the hand can be lowered as the cut deepens

Cutting Shapes

For cutting shapes either the bow-saw or the coping-saw is used. The latter is the smaller tool and is more convenient for small work. Internal cuts can be

Fig. 14. HOW BOW-SAW IS HELD

made by boring a hole through which the blade can be passed. The same thing applies to the bow-saw. This tool should be gripped by both hands as in Fig. 14.

One other tool occasionally used for internal shapes, but more generally needed for cutting the straight sides of a keyhole, is the pad- or keyhole-saw. It should be given only the minimum projection needed for the job as the blade is liable to buckle.

Unless the reader has had some experience in the work it is not advisable to sharpen his own saws. If it is attempted it is as well to start on one with big teeth. Books and leaflets on the subject are available and should be read.

Planes

Two bench planes are needed, a jack or trying plane for truing timber, and a smoothing plane for cleaning up and small work generally. For those who propose to have three planes (and this is recommended) the best selection is a wood jack plane about 15 in. with 2 in. cutter used for coarse shavings and rough work generally, a metal adjustable trying plane, 18 in. with 2⅜ in. cutter, and a metal adjustable smoothing plane 9 in. and 2 in. cutter.

For surface planing the wood is placed on the bench and is prevented from moving by the stop. At the near end the left hand should bear heavily down so that the sole is pressed flat on the wood. As it passes on to the wood the

Fig. 15. HOW PLANE IS HELD WHEN TRUING AN EDGE

pressure is equal in both, and as it reaches the far end the entire pressure is with the right hand.

When edge planing the fingers of the left hand are beneath the sole and bear against the side of the wood as in Fig. 15. They thus act as a sort of fence in preventing the plane from moving sideways. The note about transferring the pressure when surface planing applies equally, but the necessity for making the edge square has also to be considered. The edge of the cutter is slightly rounded which means that the thickest part of the shaving is in the middle. Advantage of this can be taken by adjusting the position of the plane on the wood to make an edge square. Thus if an edge is, say, high to the right the plane can be held over to this side as the shaving is thus thicker at this side. If an edge is square at one end but is out at the other the position of the plane can be altered as it passes along, thus bringing the edge true, Fig. 16.

To make an edge straight, set the trying or jointer plane fine and take shavings from the middle of the edge only until the plane ceases to remove shavings. A couple of shavings right through will then usually make the edge straight if the plane is accurate. A test should be made with the straight-edge.

For planing the edges of thin wood, say $\frac{3}{8}$ in. and less, the shooting board is invaluable. The wood is held on the upper platform with its edge overhanging about $\frac{1}{4}$ in., and the plane held on its side, and worked along the edge as in Fig. 17. It should be realized that in this operation it makes the edge straight

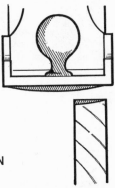

Fig. 16. HOW CURVATURE OF CUTTER (SHOWN EXAGGERATED) CAN TRUE AN EDGE

by virtue of the truth of its own sole. It does not bear against the edge of upper platform.

In the case of end trimming, however, the procedure is different. In this case the plane is held hard up against the edge of the upper platform as it is worked back and forth. A steady inward pressure is maintained on the wood against the sole of the plane which thus makes the wood square because of the squareness of the stop with the edge of the upper platform (Fig. 18). When end grain is being trimmed either the far corner of the wood must be chiselled off so that the corner does not split out, or a waste piece of wood must be held at the back to support it as in Fig. 19. Alternatively, the plane must be taken in from each direction.

When a joint is being planed on the shooting board the one piece should have its face side uppermost, and the other downwards. Then if the edge is slightly out of square, possibly owing to either the plane or the shooting board not being true, the two parts will go together in alignment since the two angles cancel each other out.

Fig. 17. PLANING AN EDGE ON SHOOTING BOARD
Note that wood overhangs so that edge is made straight by the truth of the
plane sole. Compare with Fig. 18 below

Fig. 18. TRIMMING END ON SHOOTING BOARD
Here the plane bears against the edge of the upper platform, the wood held
flush and hard against the stop

The mitre shooting board is similar but the stop is at 45 degrees. In the case of square-sectioned timber the same side of the stop can be used, the one piece being turned face side down, but with mouldings it is generally necessary to use the other side of the stop.

When planing the edges of a panel proceed in the order given in Fig. 20. Make the face edge straight (1); plane one end square with it (2); chiselling off the rear corner if necessary to prevent splitting; mark the length and plane the other end square in the same way (3); finally make the remaining edge parallel with the first (4).

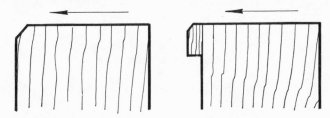

Fig. 19. AVOIDING SPLITTING OF CORNER WHEN PLANING END GRAIN

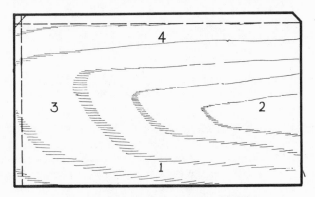

Fig. 20. ORDER OF PLANING EDGES

Sharpening and Setting the Plane

When a plane is new the cutter is ground but needs finishing on an oilstone. Remove it from the plane, tapping the front of the latter with the hammer in the case of a wood-plane, or easing the lever cap of a metal one. At the front is a back iron which is removed by slackening the bolt and sliding along the slot. The angle at which it is ground is about 25 degrees. Honing is in the region of 30 degrees. Place the cutter with the ground bevel flat on the oilstone and raise the hands slightly, this giving the approximately correct angle. Work

27

back and forth with either a straight or an elliptical movement and endeavour to keep the edge square. Slightly increased pressure at one side or the other will enable any inaccuracy to be put right. A smoothing or trying plane cutter should have its edge very slightly curved, the advantage of which has already been explained on page 24. That of the jack plane can be rather more rounded as heavier shavings are taken and it is necessary to avoid digging in at the corners. In any case, however, it is desirable to round over the corners of any bench plane. Fig. 23 shows the cutter being sharpened. The rubbing causes a burr to be formed, and this is turned back by reversing the cutter flat on the stone and rubbing once or twice. It is got rid of finally by drawing the edge across the edge of a piece of wood, then stropping on leather dressed with fine emery powder and oil.

Replace the back iron, setting it about $\frac{1}{16}$ in. from the edge, and less for the trying and smoothing planes. For difficult wood with the twisted grain it

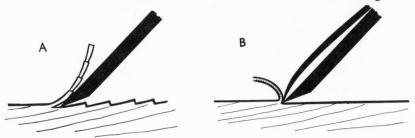

Fig. 21. WHY BACK IRON REDUCES TEARING OUT
At (A) there is no back iron. (B) has back iron fitted

should be as close to the edge as is practicable. Its whole purpose is to break the shaving as it is lifted, so robbing it of strength and preventing it from tearing out the grain. It will be realized that the reason for this tearing out is that the wood is severed or split up ahead of the actual cutting edge as shown at (A), Fig. 21. By setting the back iron close to the edge the shaving is broken almost immediately it is raised and there is thus no rigid length of shaving to cause the split.

Replace the cutter in the plane and hold it in position with the thumb of the left hand. Put in the lever cap (or wedge) and hold the plane as shown, its rear end on a light substance and look along the sole, as in Fig. 22. The cutter will appear as a thin dark line, and adjustment for thickness of cut or square-ness is made with the screw and lever. The wood plane cutter is tapped at the back with a hammer.

Rebate Planes
Quite early on the need for a rebate plane is felt, and an invaluable type is the

Fig. 22. SIGHTING PLANE

Fig. 23. SHARPENING PLANE CUTTER

adjustable metal fillister plane with fence and spur. The latter is useful when the rebate has to be worked across the grain. A depth stop is also fitted so that a rebate of constant width and depth is ensured. It is important that this plane is properly set, one essential feature being that the cutter is *slightly* proud of the side of the plane on the rebate side and that the cutter is sharpened square.

Fig. 24. HOW BADLY SET CUT-TER CAUSES REBATE PLANE TO FORM STEPS

Otherwise the result is that the plane fails to cut in square, but forms a series of small steps as shown in Fig. 24.

Another form of rebate plane, which also has many other uses, is the bull-nose, which has its cutter set near the front. It will work close up into a corner, and is so invaluable for stopped rebates. However, it is used for all sorts of jobs where close working into a corner is necessary.

Fig. 25. USING FILLISTER REBATE PLANE

Grooving Planes

Grooving also soon becomes a necessity and the metal plough plane with eight or more cutters is first choice. At a pinch it can also be used for rebating, though it is not so satisfactory for this purpose. A more elaborate tool is the universal plane, which has several moulding cutters in addition to those for grooving and rebating. For those who do only occasional grooving the small grooving plane with three cutters, $\frac{1}{8}$ in., $\frac{3}{16}$ in., $\frac{1}{4}$ in., is perfectly effective. It has both fence and depth stop.

In use both the grooving and the rebate plane should be started at the far end of the wood as in Fig. 25. A few short strokes are made, and the plane brought a little farther back at each successive stroke. In this way the plane tends to keep in the groove (or rebate) it has already made. Otherwise it may drift from the edge. In any case a constant inward pressure is maintained so that the fence is kept hard up against the side of the wood. It will cease to cut when the finished depth is reached as the stop comes into operation.

When sharpening grooving and rebate planes it is essential that the cutting edge is made straight and square. The same applies to the shoulder and bull-nose planes. These are used with the bevel uppermost.

Router and Spokeshave

The hand router is used to bring grooves and other recesses to an even depth. The metal type cuts more easily in that the cutter is set at an angle and approaches the wood with more of a chisel action. On the other hand, the wood router will work in a more confined area as Fig. 26 makes clear. Its action is that of scraping rather than cutting.

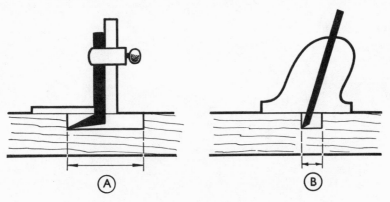

Fig. 26. COMPARISON OF METAL (A) AND WOOD ROUTERS

Fig. 27. FILING EDGE OF SCRAPER

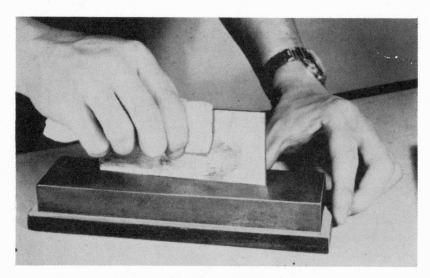

Fig. 28. RUBBING DOWN EDGE OF SCRAPER

Spokeshaves are of two main kinds—wood and metal. The latter can be either round-faced for hollow shapes, or flat for convex curves. Choice is largely personal preference. Often it is a help to hold the tool at an angle so that it makes a slicing cut. The metal kind is sharpened much as a plane cutter, a special holder with a saw cut in it being used to grip the cutter. For the wood type the oilstone is turned on its edge or an oilstone slip used. Generally the tool cuts better if the burr is not removed.

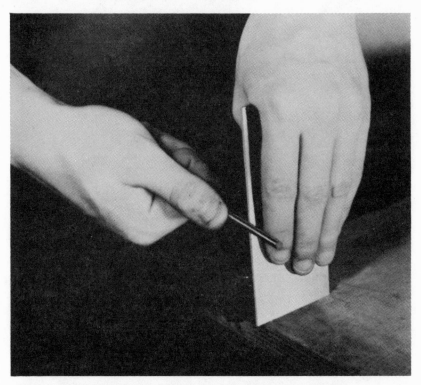

Fig. 29. HOW EDGE OF SCRAPER IS TURNED

Scrapers

For those who do cabinet work a scraper is essential. It serves two purposes; to remove marks made by the plane, and to take out tears (pronounced 'tares') in the grain. Some woods are liable to tear out in parts no matter which way they are planed, and the scraper is the only means of removing such blemishes. Some people have difficulty in sharpening it, but there is

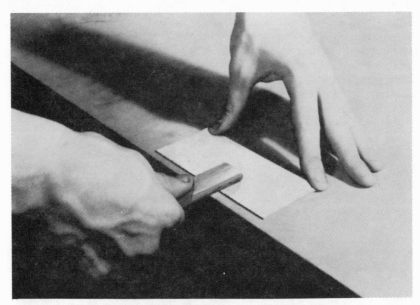

Fig. 30. TURNING BACK EDGE OF SCRAPER

Fig. 31. HOW SCRAPER IS HELD

really little in it. Fix the scraper in the vice and with a flat file (medium or fine cut) file each long edge straight and square as in Fig. 27, making sure that there are no dull, rounded edges. Finish off on the oilstone (Fig. 28), holding the scraper in rag so that the hand is not injured. Rub it back and forth in all directions on the stone until all file marks are taken out. Finish off by rubbing each side flat on the stone.

Now comes the actual turning of the edge. Hold the scraper so that it overhangs the edge of the bench about $\frac{1}{4}$ in. and draw a hard rounded tool such as a ticketer (or a gouge will do) along the edge at an angle of about 80–85 degrees. If the thumb is drawn across the flat of the scraper a distinct turned-up edge should be apparent. Treat all four edges alike. Some workers prefer to hold the scraper upright on the bench and draw the ticketer upwards as in Fig. 29.

When the tool becomes dull the edge can be turned back by holding the scraper flat on the bench and drawing the ticketer flat on the side once or twice (Fig. 30). It is then a matter of turning up the edge afresh. It can be resharpened in this way two or three times, but eventually it is necessary to rub down again with file and oilstone and start afresh.

In use the tool is held at an angle (found by experiment) and gripped as in Fig. 31. Thus the tool is slightly bent by pressure from the thumbs and there is no tendency to dig in with the corners. The most awkward part is when starting at the near end of the wood, and the simplest way generally is to hold the tool askew so that one end of it already bears on the wood. Some difficult woods, notably the woolly varieties, tend to tear out no matter in which direction they are scraped, and it is then a matter of dealing with each tear locally. Some woods are best dealt with by scraping in each direction.

Chiselling

This is generally of two kinds: paring and chopping. The former calls for a really keen edge, and may be with the chisel used horizontally or vertically according to circumstances. The wood may be held in the vice or fixed down with a cramp. A typical example of paring is in cutting a notch as in Fig. 32 The sides are sawn across the grain first. If the notch does not run right across the wood it is only possible to saw down as far as the diagonal, as in Fig. 33. The rest is chopped down with the chisel as the work proceeds.

For the preliminary cuts the chisel may be tapped with the mallet or thumped with the ball of the hand and, to avoid splitting out, the cuts can be taken in from each side as in Fig. 34. To finish off the chisel is used with a slicing action, and if properly used will tend to make the surface flat by virtue of its flatness. It automatically removes the high parts. Note, from Fig. 32, how the thumb of the left hand bears down on the chisel.

In vertical paring the thumb of the right hand is invariably over the top of the handle, as in Fig. 35, and the fingers of the left hand curl around the blade to guide and steady it. Here, as in all chiselling operations, both hands are behind the cutting edge.

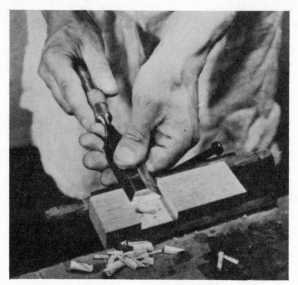

Fig. 32. PARING HALVING WITH CHISEL

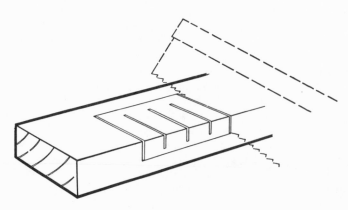

Fig. 33. CUTTING STOPPED NOTCH

Examples of chopping with the chisel are in dovetailing and mortising. The mallet is used, and clearly a robustly built tool is necessary. A point to realize at the outset is that, owing to its wedge shape, there is a tendency for

Fig. 34. STAGES IN
CUTTING HALVING

the chisel to spread beyond the line up to which it is to cut unless certain precautions are taken. The simplest plan is to make the first cut well short of the line (A, Fig. 36), and remove some of the waste wood by a cut at the end *with* the grain (B). Then when the final cut is made right up to the line there

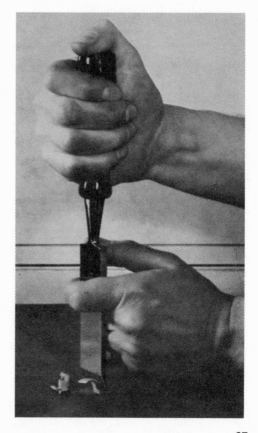

Fig. 35. HOLDING
CHISEL WHEN
PARING A CORNER

is no tendency for the wood to be compressed beyond the line because the narrow waste piece curls away easily as at (C). Much the same applies to mortising, but both this and dovetail cutting are dealt with more fully in the chapter on cutting joints.

Gouges are not widely used in general woodwork, and it is better to buy one only when the need is felt. There are two kinds; firmer which has the bevel at the outside, and scribing with the bevel inside. The former is a general-purpose tool and is sharpened by holding it at right-angles with the oilstone and partly revolving it as it is moved back and forth. Any burr at the inside is turned back by using an oilstone slip. Scribing gouges need an oil-

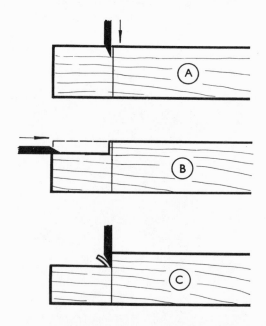

Fig. 36. CHOPPING A REBATE AT THE END OF WOOD

stone slip to sharpen the inside bevel, and the slip should be of the same curvature as the gouge or slightly quicker. It takes a long time to sharpen well and the edge should be protected from damage.

Sharpening the chisel is similar to the plane cutter, Fig. 23, but, as it is much narrower, its position on the oilstone should be varied so that the stone is not worn unevenly.

Boring Tools

The advantage of the ratchet brace is that it can be used close to a wall or in a corner, being moved through part of its stroke only. Furthermore, in the case of a large hole which offers considerable resistance, the brace can be moved back and forth in the easiest part of the stroke—generally the pull stroke.

It is usually obvious whether the brace leans to left or right, but more

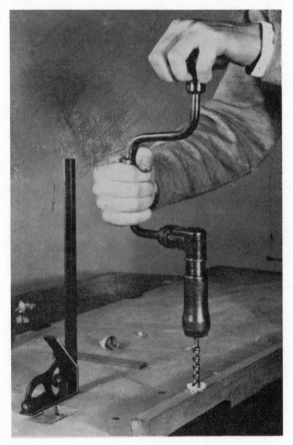

Fig. 37. AID TO VERTICAL BORING

difficult to detect whether it bears away from or towards one. As a guide a square can be placed near the bit, as in Fig. 37, but in a really important case it is helpful to ask an assistant to stand at one side and indicate whether the brace is upright.

Sometimes verticality is more important in one direction than in another, and the obvious thing is to stand in the most favourable position. An example is when boring holes in a mortise to partly remove the waste. Clearly the holes must not bear across the wood, whereas a slight leaning along the length would not matter. Consequently it is desirable to stand at the end of a rail when boring rather than at the side.

In some special cases it is necessary to make a jig to ensure that the hole

Fig. 38. DOWELLING JIG IN USE
This can also be used as a guide to vertical boring

is accurate, this being cramped to the wood. Thus in the case of a dowelled joint a special jig is a great help. The specially made dowelling jig is cramped on and ensures truth (see Fig. 38).

When a hole has to be bored right through wood it is generally necessary to bore half-way in from each side. In the case of thin wood the bit is taken in until the centre point emerges beneath, when the wood is reversed.

The centre bit is suitable only for shallow holes as it is liable to wander with the grain. For deeper holes, such as when dowelling, the twist-bit is used. Sometimes a hole has to be bored to a definite depth, or several holes all to the same depth. For this a depth gauge should be used, either the specially made metal type which can be fixed at any point along the bit, or the simple home-made type as at (A) and (B), Fig. 39. The length of (A) is made to suit the length of bit being used.

Take care to avoid jabbing the point of the twist-bit on other metal tools, and in particular on nails embedded in the wood. The thread is easily damaged, and cannot usually be put right if badly fouled. The cutters and nickers can be sharpened with a fine file, but there is a limit to the number of times they can be filed, and it is clearly better to avoid accidental damage. When filing a bit stick the screw point in to a waste block of wood, and use a file with a safe edge. For cutters file the underside only, that is, the side away from the screw thread. The nickers are sharpened inside.

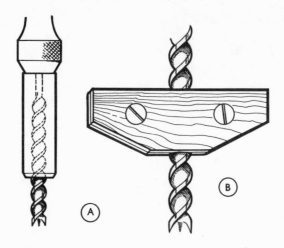

Fig. 39. TWO DEPTH GAUGES

Gauges

Gauges are a necessity in all woodwork, partly for marking widths and thicknesses parallel with a true surface, and for fixing fittings. The two chief kinds are the marking gauge used for lines in the same direction as the grain, and the cutting gauge which may be used for marking either across or with the grain, or for the cutting thin wood, veneer, etc. Some fittings call for the use

41

Fig. 40. HOW GAUGE SHOULD BE HELD

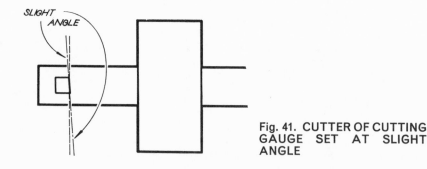

Fig. 41. CUTTER OF CUTTING GAUGE SET AT SLIGHT ANGLE

of two gauges—hinges, for example—and the reader is advised to obtain one marking and one cutting gauge.

The tool calls for care in its use to avoid merely drifting with the grain. It is held as in Fig. 40 in which the downward pressure is exerted largely by the first finger, the forward movement by the thumb and root of the first finger, and the inward pressure to keep the fence up to the edge of the wood by the second finger. This latter pressure is most important whether the gauge tends to drift with the grain or not. It is advisable to file the surface against which the cutter beds so that it is at a slight angle, as shown in Fig. 41. Thus it tends to pull the fence up to the edge of the wood, though it is still necessary to maintain a strong inward pressure.

The mortise gauge is similar to the marking gauge, except that it has two markers, one of which is adjustable. It is used almost entirely for marking mortises and tenons, and since the mortise has to be chopped with a chisel of definite width the markers of the gauge are set exactly to the chisel width. The fence is then set so that the markers are central of the wood, or in whatever

Fig. 42. TESTING SQUARENESS OF REBATE

position may be required. In use the fence is worked against the face side or edge of the wood in every case.

Another tool essential for marking and testing is the try-square. Apart from being equally useful for all purposes for which the fixed square is used, the sliding square is invaluable for testing rebates, notches, etc. as shown in Fig. 42. A large wood-square is useful and indeed necessary for big jobs, and this is among the items that can usefully be made.

Another item that should be made is the straight-edge, which should be in a reliable hardwood.

2 Joints

THERE IS A huge variety of joints designed for various purposes, but those in this chapter will cover most requirements.

EDGE JOINTS

These are used when it is necessary to join two or more pieces together to obtain the required width. In the simplest form the joint is planed true and

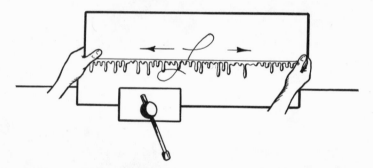

Fig. 1. PARTS OF GLUED JOINT RUBBED TOGETHER

the two parts rub-glued together; that is, the one piece is fixed in the vice, the other placed alongside and both joining edges glued simultaneously. The one is straightway erected in position and rubbed back and forth to squeeze out surplus glue and bring the two into close contact. A short joint up to about 2 ft. or so can be rubbed without assistance, but a long one calls for someone at each end. When Scotch glue is used the parts should be warmed beforehand so that the glue is not chilled by cold wood. Fig. 1 shows a joint being rubbed.

Planing the Joint
Wood of about $\frac{1}{2}$ in. or more thickness can be planed in the vice, but thinner wood is better dealt with on the shooting board, the one piece face side upper-

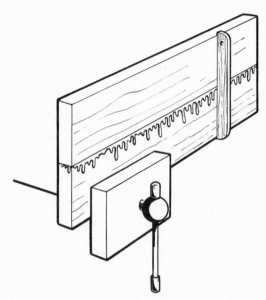

**Fig. 2. TESTING
ALIGNMENT OF
GLUED JOINT**

most, and the other downwards so that the two go together in alignment. When being tried together for accuracy the two parts should fit closely along the entire length. On no account should the joint pivot freely on the middle. Test by a swivelling action. There should be definite friction at the ends. Another essential test is to see that the parts are in alignment. The straight-edge is used for this as in Fig. 2.

The joint, having been glued, can be lifted bodily from the vice, and rested against a sloping oddment of wood as in Fig. 3. When two joints are needed in a panel, the middle piece is put in the vice and the top one rubbed to it. The

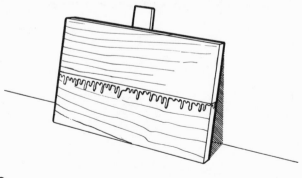

**Fig. 3. JOINT
STACKED
WHILST SETTING**

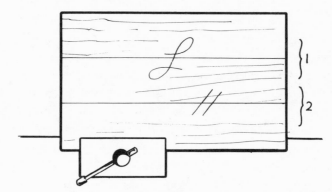

Fig. 4. JOINTS ERECTED ONE ABOVE THE OTHER

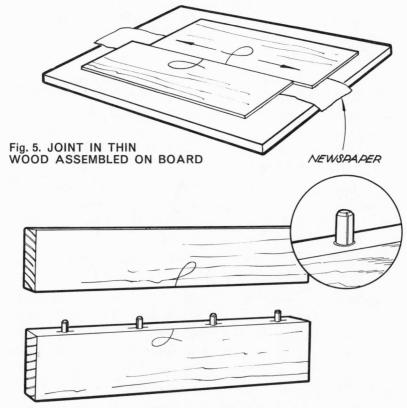

Fig. 5. JOINT IN THIN
WOOD ASSEMBLED ON BOARD

NEWSPAPER

Fig. 6. JOINT STRENGTHENED WITH DOWELS

remaining piece is then held in the vice and the previously glued pair rubbed as a whole (see Fig. 4).

When the wood is really thin it is obvious that the parts could not be glued in the vice as the top one would topple over. They are, therefore, put together on a flat board as in Fig. 5, a piece of newspaper being placed on the board so that the parts do not stick to the latter.

When an accurate machine planer in good condition is available this can be used for joints, but the short planer often used in the small workshop is seldom long enough except for short joints, and some of them are not accurate enough. In the latter case the best plan is to pass the wood over the machine planer to remove the rough and make it square and reasonably straight, and finish with the hand plane.

Methods of Strengthening

On good gluing woods and those not liable to be subjected to strain the plain rubbed joint is satisfactory. It can be strengthened, however, by dowelling,

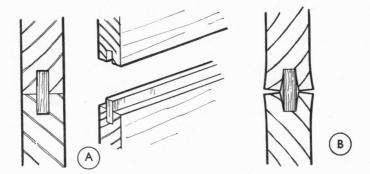

Fig. 7. THE TONGUED EDGE JOINT
Result of tight tongue is shown at (B)

tonguing, or slot-screwing. In all cases the preliminary planing is the same. For dowels the parts are cramped together temporarily and the dowel positions squared across both edges. A gauge is set to the middle of the wood, and each pencil line cut from the face side. The holes are bored and lightly countersunk, and the cut-off dowels glued into one piece. It helps in assembling if the ends of the dowels are lightly chamfered (Fig. 6). Each should have a saw cut along the length to enable surplus glue to escape. The purpose of the light countersinking is to allow for any accumulation of glue around the dowel which might otherwise prevent the joint from going tightly together.

The tongued and grooved joint is the strongest, but shows at the ends unless the grooves are stopped. The best proportions are shown at (A), Fig. 7.

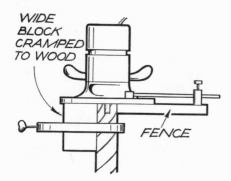

Fig. 8. GROOVING EDGE
WITH ROUTER
Block is cramped to the wood

A thicker tongue results in the wood at each side being rather thin. The grain of the tongue should run crosswise or at about 45 degrees. Plywood is frequently used. It should be a comfortable finger-tight fit. If too tight it will tend to force the sides of the groove open as at (B).

The method of cutting the grooves depends upon the facilities available. If the hand plough or grooving plane is used the grooves will have to be taken right through. Remember to use the tool from the face side in both pieces. Another way of grooving is to use the circular saw. An 8-in. or 9-in. saw with rip or cross-cut teeth will generally cut a groove of suitable width in one pass. It is usually necessary to take it right through because the size of the saw involves a rather long run-out curve.

The router is an excellent means of grooving. The most convenient way is to fix the machine beneath the table and move the wood across it against a fence. If this is not practicable some means of preventing tilting is desirable, necessitated by the narrow bearing surface of the edge of the wood. Either a piece of wood can be fixed at one side to increase the width, Fig. 8, or a wide upright can be fixed to the sole of the router, Fig. 9. One advantage of the electric router is that the groove can be stopped if necessary. Another method is to use the spindle moulder.

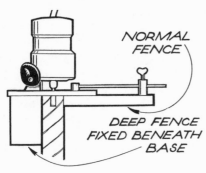

Fig. 9. ALTERNATIVE
METHOD OF EDGE
GROOVING
Block or fence is fixed beneath
router sole

When cold glue is used, the entire assembling can be in a single operation, but hot Scotch glue generally necessitates the tongue being glued to the piece first, as otherwise the glue is chilled before cramping can be completed. With a short or medium joint it would be practicable, the parts being heated and the assembling done in a warm shop. As in the case of the dowelled joint cramping is essential.

Slot screwing is sometimes used. The screw positions are squared across the edges and marked with the gauge. That which is to receive the screw head is offset about $\frac{1}{8}$ in. Screws are driven into the one piece, and holes to

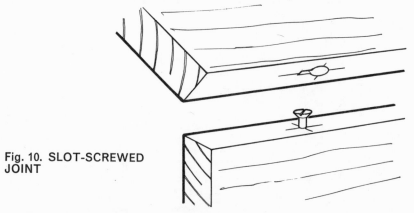

Fig. 10. SLOT-SCREWED JOINT

take the heads are bored in the other. A slot is cut at one side to enable the screw shank to move sideways, as in Fig. 10. The parts are cramped together dry, the cramps at a slight angle, and the one piece knocked with the mallet until the two are level. It is then knocked apart, and the screws tightened half a turn. The joint is glued and put together as before. Note that the angularity of the cramps helps in knocking the top piece into position.

MORTISE AND TENON JOINTS

For doors, framings, etc., the mortise and tenon joint is the most widely used. It varies in detail, but basically the one piece has a projecting part (the tenon) which fits into a corresponding recess (the mortise). Generally the width of the mortise is one-third that of the thickness of the wood, but in practice the mortise width equals that of the chisel used to chop the mortise, this being as nearly the one-third size as possible. Thus for $\frac{3}{4}$ in. wood the chisel is $\frac{1}{4}$ in.; for $\frac{7}{8}$ in. stuff it is $\frac{5}{16}$ in.; and for $1\frac{1}{4}$ in. wood, $\frac{3}{8}$ in.

Variations of the Joints

Its simplest form is shown in Fig. 11. The haunch is sometimes omitted, but

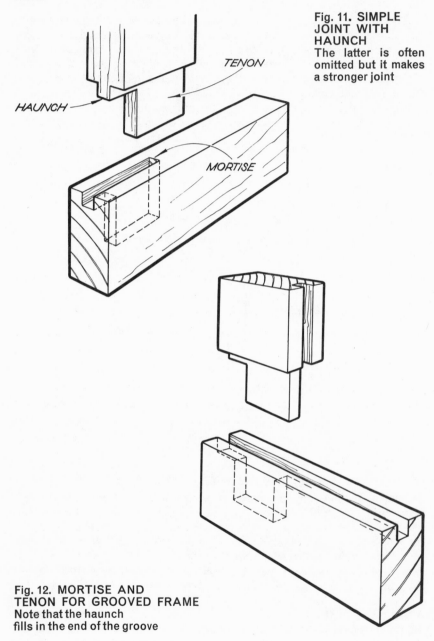

TENON

HAUNCH

MORTISE

Fig. 11. SIMPLE
JOINT WITH
HAUNCH
The latter is often
omitted but it makes
a stronger joint

Fig. 12. MORTISE AND
TENON FOR GROOVED FRAME
Note that the haunch
fills in the end of the groove

Fig. 13. JOINT FOR REBATED
FRAME
The haunch is advisable though
it is sometimes omitted

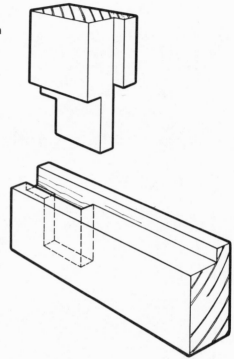

it does strengthen the joint, preventing any tendency to twist sideways. When
the framework is grooved to take a panel the groove passes along the length of
both pieces, and a haunch is essential to fill in the end of the groove. As the
groove necessarily removes part of the inner side of the tenon, the length of
the mortise must be curtailed by this amount as shown in Fig. 12.

In the case of a rebated frame, the rebate, in being taken right through,
necessarily cuts away part of both the mortised piece and the tenon. Consequently the back shoulder which reaches into the rebate has to be longer than
the other by the rebate depth. Furthermore, since the rebate removes one
edge of the tenon the mortise length has to be curtailed by the same amount.
These details are shown in Fig. 13. In the best work a haunch is cut at the
tenon though it is frequently omitted.

An exception to the necessity of long and short shoulders is when either a
spindle moulder or a router is used to work the rebate *after* the frame has been
assembled. In this case a simple square-edged frame is made and the rebating
worked afterwards. This will leave rounded corners which have to be cut in
square by hand afterwards. The idea is shown in Fig. 14.

Another type of framework often used in cabinet work is both moulded and rebated as in Fig. 15. In this, the shoulders are level, the moulding being cut away locally at the mortise. Note that the bottom quirk of the moulding is level with the rebate so that when the moulding is cut away a level surface is formed. It will be realized that the shoulder length has to be increased by rebate depth. This is made clear in Fig. 16. The procedure is to complete the jointing first, work the rebate and the moulding, and mitre the latter last, using a mitre template and chisel (Fig. 17).

In machine shops the moulding is taken right through on both pieces, and a special cutter fitted to the tenoner which cuts a reverse of the moulding at

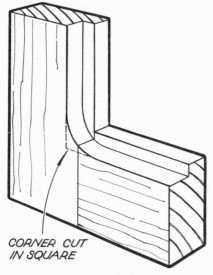

CORNER CUT
IN SQUARE

Fig. 14. JOINT WHEN REBATE IS MACHINED AFTER ASSEMBLY
The rounded corner has to be cut square by hand

the shoulder. Thus the moulding is scribed which gives an almost identical appearance to the mitre. For cheap work a simple square-edged frame is made and a separate moulding mitred round, thus forming a rebate, as in Fig. 18. The moulding is glued and pinned. The same idea is followed when a bolection moulding is required. This is rebated and projects from the face of the framework, Fig. 19.

Chopping Mortises

The method of cutting the mortise and tenon joint depends upon the facilities available. If the entire work is to be by hand methods, the mortise position is squared across the edge of the wood in pencil, and the mortise gauge set to the width of the chisel being used. Extra length is always allowed as waste at

**Fig. 15.
MOULDED
AND REBATED
FRAME JOINT**

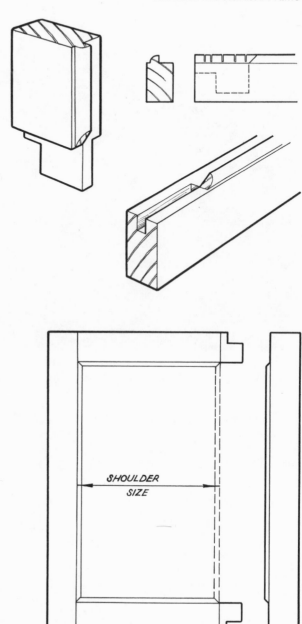

**Fig. 16. HOW
SHOULDER SIZE
IS CALCULATED
FOR JOINT IN
Fig. 15**

SHOULDER
SIZE

Fig. 17. MITRING STUCK MOULDING WITH MITRE TEMPLATE
The left thumb usually bears on the chisel, but is not so shown as it would
hide the detail

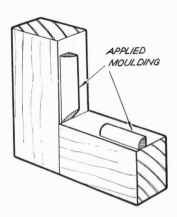

APPLIED MOULDING

**Fig. 18. FRAME WITH
APPLIED MOULDING**

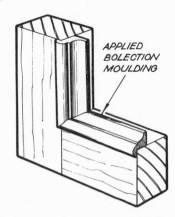

APPLIED BOLECTION MOULDING

Fig. 19. FRAME WITH BOLECTION MOULDING

the end so that any tendency to split out is lessened. Much of the waste can be removed by boring a series of holes using a bit slightly smaller than the mortise ($\frac{1}{4}$ in. for a $\frac{5}{16}$ in. mortise). Stand at the end of the wood because it is important that the mortises do not tend to slope out towards the sides, Fig. 20. Start the chisel about the middle, and work first in one direction, then the

Fig. 20. CHOPPING MORTISES OF FRAMEWORK

other, deepening the mortise as the ends are approached. It helps if the waste is levered out, but, as this has the effect of rounding over the ends, the final cuts at the ends should be made only after the levering has been completed. A piece of paper or Sellotape stuck to the side of the chisel will indicate when the full depth has been reached.

Always do this chopping over a solid part of the bench, and put a cramp over the thickness of the wood to avoid splitting out (it is also to help in this respect that the extra length is allowed). It is obvious that the mortise must be parallel with the side of the wood, and it is therefore helpful to stand at the end as it is easy to tell whether the chisel leans to left or right.

Tenons

The tenons' shoulders should be squared round with knife or chisel, and the tenon marked with the mortise gauge at the same setting. Hold the wood at an

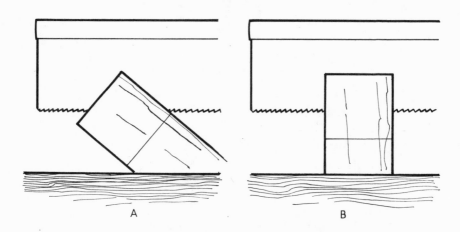

Fig. 21. SAWING TENON, WOOD HELD IN VICE
First cut is at (A). Wood is then reversed, this time upright, and the cut completed

angle in the vice and saw down as far as the diagonal, as in Fig. 21, just leaving the gauge marks in. Then reverse the wood in the vice, this time upright, and complete the saw cuts. Before sawing the shoulders, make a sloping groove on the waste side of the squared cut with the chisel, as in Fig. 22, thus forming a channel in which the saw can run.

When fitting the joints it is as well to keep the cramp on the end of the stile to avoid any possibility of splitting the wood in the event of the tenon being too tight. Two chief tests are necessary. The tenoned piece should be in alignment with the other as revealed by a straight-edge or square (A, Fig. 23); and it should not be twisted (B). Either faults can cause a framework to be in winding as in Fig. 24.

Fig. 22. CHISEL CUT AT
SHOULDER TO GUIDE
SAW

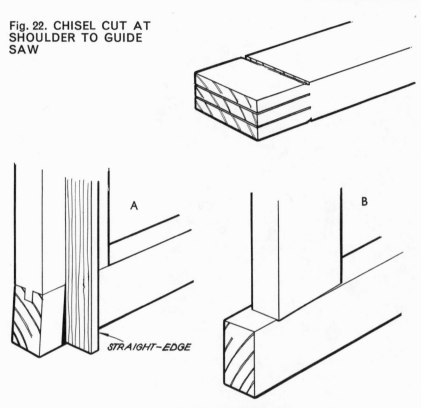

Fig. 23. FAULTS IN MORTISE AND TENON JOINT
At (A) parts are out of alignment. At (B) the rail twists

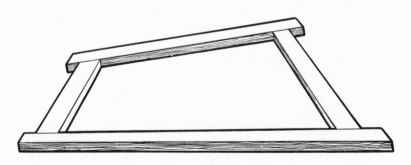

Fig. 24. FRAMEWORK IN WINDING

Use of Circular Saw

When a circular saw is available this is the ideal means of sawing tenons. A special jig is made up, as in Fig. 25, this working up against the fence. Small pieces can be held against the jig by hand and the whole pushed forward.

Fig. 25. CUTTING TENON ON CIRCULAR SAW

Larger pieces can be fixed to the jig with a thumbscrew. Remember to hold the wood with the face side against the jig in every case. One side of all tenons is sawn first, then the second side of all. The saw is first set to the required height (the tenon length), and the fence so adjusted that the saw just leaves the gauge marks in. It will be obvious that wood must be cut square dead to length beforehand as otherwise some cuts may be short of the shoulder line and others may overrun.

An alternative method is to use the band-saw for tenoning. A fence is fixed to the table and the wood sawn on its edge, as in Fig. 26. In this case exact cutting to length beforehand is not essential because the cut can be stopped as the shoulder is reached. Incidentally, it may be noted that there is no

Fig. 26. TENON SAWN ON BAND-SAW

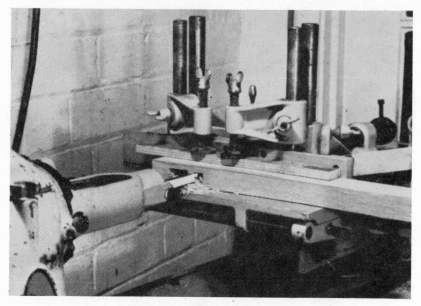

Fig. 27. HOLLOW CHISEL MORTISER IN USE

need to gauge the tenons of all the pieces whether the circular or the band-saw is used. One only need be marked and the machine set to this. The others are bound to be exactly the same. The shoulders need to be marked, and for cabinet work should be hand-cut with a back-saw as the machine-saw finish is too coarse. For rough carpentry, however, the machine-saw can be used.

Machine Mortising

Mortises can be cut with either the hollow chisel and auger, or the rotary miller bit. The former, shown in use in Fig. 27, cuts square ends to the mortise, and works in a series of stabs, the square chisel cutting the corners and the auger removing the waste. To set the machine, fix the chisel so that there is a gap of about $\frac{1}{16}$ in. at the shoulder (Fig. 28). Insert the auger so that it goes

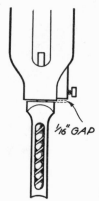

Fig. 28. HOW HOLLOW CHISEL AND AUGER ARE SET

in as far as it will, and tighten the chuck which grips it. Free the chisel and press it home so that the shoulder is tight.

Both blind and through mortises can be cut. In the latter case a waste piece of wood is placed beneath that being mortised. This is partly to protect the tool which would otherwise be damaged by fouling the metal bed of the machine, and also to support the underside of the wood which would otherwise be liable to splinter out beneath. The haunch recess can be cut on the same machine, the movement being restricted by setting the stop accordingly.

Most individual mortisers work vertically, the chisel being pressed down into the wood. Mortising attachments for a lathe, however, work horizontally, the wood being moved up to the chisel. The principle of cutting is exactly the same, however.

The rotary miller bit works in a different way. This bit can cut either sideways or in line with its length. What happens is that the revolving bit is entered into the wood, and either it or the latter moved sideways so that the length of the mortise is completed. It is not practicable to take the bit into the full depth and then shift sideways as the strain would be too great. Instead it is taken in about $\frac{1}{4}$ in. to $\frac{1}{2}$ in. (depending on the hardness of the wood), the length completed, and the process repeated until the full depth is reached. Fig. 29 shows the rotary miller bit in use.

In another way a series of stabs down to the full depth is made and then the remaining waste cleared by the lateral movement. Here, again, the haunch recess can be cut, but to save having to re-set the machine every time, it is better to complete all the mortises, re-set the machine, and put the parts through a second time for the haunch recesses.

Fig. 29. MORTISING WITH ROTARY MILLER BIT

It will be realized that the ends of the mortises are necessarily rounded, and for cabinet work these have to be cut square by hand. In rough carpentry, however, they can be left, and the sides of the tenons rounded over with rasp or shaper tool. One other advantage of the rotary miller bit method is that grooves along the length of rails can be cut with it. In this case the wood is not fixed on the carriage but is passed along by hand. The direction of movement is important as otherwise the wood is liable to jump and cause a false cut. It should be in a direction so that the down-coming cutting edge presses the wood down on to the carriage platform.

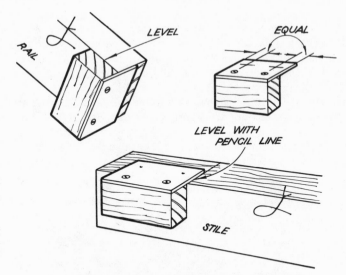

Fig. 30. DEVICE FOR MARKING DOWELS

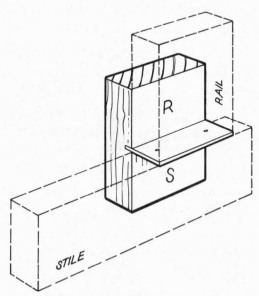

Fig. 31. ALTERNATIVE APPLIANCE

Dowelled Joints

An alternative to the mortise and tenon often used to reduce costs is the dowelled joint. In machine shops, in particular, it is widely used since by means of fences and stops it is only a case of pushing the wood up to the revolving drill. In handwork, marking out and boring is necessary but it is still quicker than tenoning though not so satisfactory.

Various methods can be adopted for marking out. For one or two odd joints the positions can be squared across the one piece, transferred to the other, and again squared across. A gauge mark from the face side cut across each line gives the exact dowel positions. In another way the simple device in Fig. 30 can be used. This is simply a metal plate screwed to the square edge of a piece of wood, and having drilled in it small holes giving the dowel hole

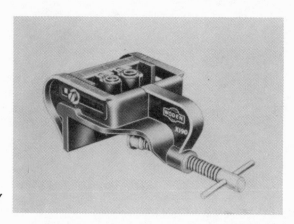

Fig. 32. PROPRIETARY
DOWELLING DEVICE

positions. The marking awl is pressed into each hole in turn. Since the device is necessarily reversed when marking the end of the rail as compared with the side of the stile, it is clearly essential that the two marking holes are exactly the same distance from the ends of the metal plate. An alternative form of marker which gets over this necessity is that in Fig. 31. Here the end marked R is put at the end of the rail and that marked S over the stile. Thus the marking is in the same relative position in both pieces.

Alternatively, the dowelling jig shown in Fig. 32 can be used. This not only gives the exact position but enables the holes to be bored square.

When dowels have to be entered at an angle, the most satisfactory way is to make a special jig. Bore the guiding hole through the wood and cut off the end at the required angle. A fence is fixed to the side at the same angle as the cut-off end, and this fixed with a cramp to the side of the wood. The idea is

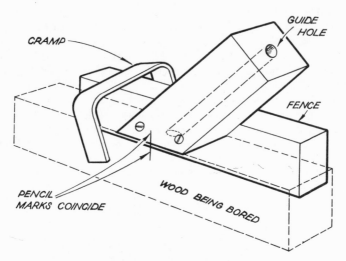

Fig. 33. JIG FOR BORING AT AN ANGLE

shown in Fig. 33. A line squared across the end of the jig in line with the hole and squared up at the side is brought in line with a mark at the side of the wood being bored.

HALVING JOINTS

These (Fig. 34) can be of the X type where two members cross each other; the L form used at the corner of a framework; and the T joint where the end of one piece meets the centre of another. In addition, any of the three types can meet at any odd angle. It has not much mechanical strength in that the two have to be screwed as well as glued together, but is often used in positions in which the screw heads do not matter. Thus, loose seat frames of chairs are often halved.

The L type can be cut entirely with the saw. Depth marking out is done with the gauge from the face side and the cut made immediately to the waste side, whether cut by hand or on the circular-saw. In X and T joints the chisel is used to pare away the waste after the ends have been sawn. In machine work the router can be used for the notch, or even the circular saw, though in the latter case several passes have to be made as the saw only removes its own saw kerf at each pass.

In the case of hand work the ends are sawn down to the gauge line, and the waste removed from one side with the chisel as far as the diagonal (A,

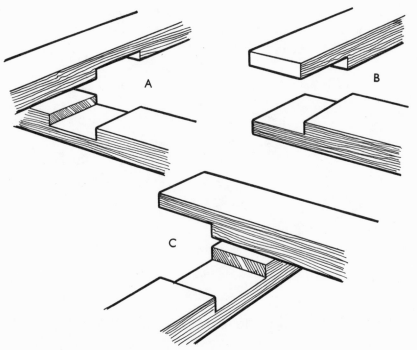

Fig. 34. CROSS HALVING (A), L HALVING (B), T HALVING (C)

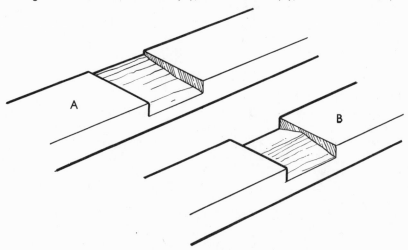

Fig. 35. STAGES IN CUTTING HALVING

Fig. 35). It is then reversed and the notch pared away until flat (B). It will be found that the wood finishes more smoothly in one direction than in the other, especially some softwoods, and it is as well to finish off in this direction.

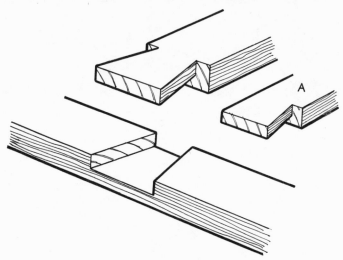

Fig. 36. DOVETAIL HALVING, BAREFACED JOINT SHOWN AT (A)

The dovetail halving (Fig. 36) is useful for some work in that it resists any outward stress. To cut this the halving on the dovetailed piece is cut first, then the slope of the dovetail. This is laid in position on the piece with the socket and the sides marked.

DOVETAILS

Through Dovetail

The simplest form of dovetail is the through type (Fig. 37) used when it is concealed, or when there is no objection to its appearance. The first essential is to plane the edges of the joining pieces straight and square. A cutting gauge is then set to the thickness of the one piece and the other marked with it, and the process repeated with the other as in Fig. 38. Often, of course, both pieces are of the same thickness. Mark in only lightly. Now pencil in lightly the dovetail positions.

In an important job these are spaced exactly and the slope drawn in with either an adjustable bevel or a dovetail marker. This slope is usually $\frac{1}{2}$ in. or $\frac{5}{8}$ in. in 3 in. (see Fig. 37). In a commercial job one has not the time for exact spacing, and in any case the man who is used to it is able to judge the spacing

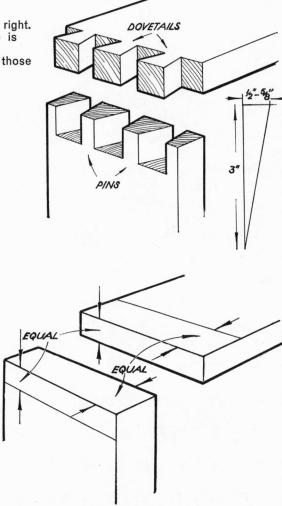

Fig. 37. THROUGH DOVETAILS
Angle is shown to the right. The less acute slope is generally used for hardwoods, especially those which show

Fig. 38. GAUGING THROUGH DOVETAILS

with extraordinary accuracy. The same thing applies to the slope. The tradesman knows the angle from long usage. For the less experienced man a better plan is to fix the wood in the vice so that the required cut is vertical. The idea is shown in Fig. 39 which shows the slope adjusted to a try-square rested upon the vice. Cut down each line in turn.

From this point the procedure may vary according to the method to be

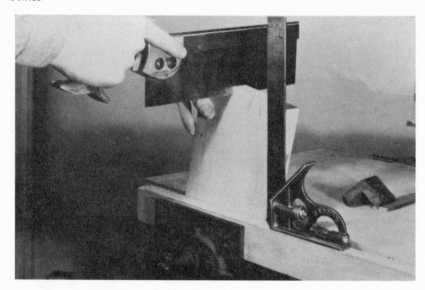

Fig. 39. SAWING DOVETAILS, WOOD HELD SLOPING IN VICE

Fig. 40. TRANSFERRING MARKS TO PINS WITH SAW

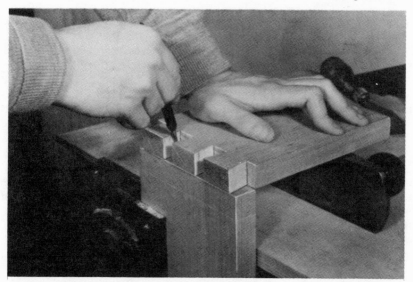

Fig. 41. AWL USED TO TRANSFER DOVETAIL MARKS TO PINS

used for transferring the marks to the other piece. The method widely used in the trade is to lay the piece in position on the edge of the other, the far end supported on a block. Pressure is applied with one hand, and the saw placed in each kerf in turn and drawn back, so marking the pins as in Fig. 40. The latter are cut with the saw held immediately to the waste side.

The alternative method, and one which is advisable for the less experienced man, is to remove the waste from the dovetailed piece, lay it in position as before, and mark round with a marking awl (Fig. 41). Again the saw is held to the waste side when cutting the pins.

To remove the waste of both tails and pins, a coping-saw should be used, cutting within a bare $\frac{1}{16}$ in. of the gauge line. The remainder is then chiselled away. A quicker trade method is to chop down with the chisel only, half-way

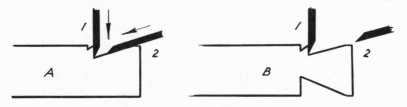

Fig. 42. STAGES IN CHOPPING DOVETAILS

from each side, but unless precautions are taken the grain is liable to be wrenched out at the middle of the shoulders. To avoid this, chop down about $\frac{1}{16}$ in. from the gauge line and make a sloping cut to meet it as in Fig. 42. A second cut is then made right on the gauge line (unless the first cut is away from the gauge line the chisel is liable to be forced beyond the shoulder), and a second sloping cut made. The wood is now reversed and the process repeated. It will be realized that the reason for the wood being torn out is that the downward blow causes the waste piece to be bent downward, so fracturing the grain. The sloping cut prevents this since an uncut portion is left to bed down. In any case a keen chisel is essential.

Two points to note are that the work is placed on a flat waste piece, and is cramped down over a solid part of the bench. Before putting together, the inner edges of the dovetails should be eased off with a chisel from a point just inside the corners as in Fig. 43. It eases the parts in starting. Generally, dovetails should not be put together dry as it loosens them. They should just be offered together to see that they are satisfactory and not assembled until glued. Note that a waste batten is placed over the joint when being knocked

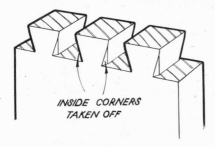

INSIDE CORNERS
TAKEN OFF

Fig. 43. DOVETAILS EASED FOR ASSEMBLING

home to avoid bruising and to spread the force of the blow and so avoid splitting the wood. Incidentally, the pins can be cut first if preferred, and the dovetails marked from them with the awl.

Lapped Dovetails
These are used when it is necessary to conceal the joint at one side. Thus, in a cabinet, wardrobe, etc., the top and bottom are usually lap-dovetailed to the ends as the joint cannot be seen at the sides (Fig. 44). In a job of this kind the ends are trimmed to the finished over-all size, but the top and bottom are shorter by the combined thickness of the two laps. They may also have to be narrower if the ends are rebated to hold the back.

To mark the joint, set the cutting gauge to the thickness of the top and mark across the inner face of the end. Now set a gauge to the dovetail length (which is the thickness of the end, less the lap) and mark both sides of the top. Fig. 45 shows the idea. The procedure of marking and cutting is the same

Fig. 44. LAPPED DOVETAIL

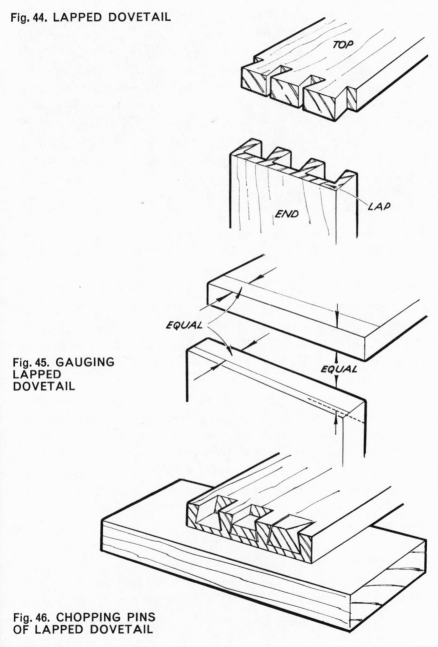

TOP

END

LAP

EQUAL

EQUAL

Fig. 45. GAUGING LAPPED DOVETAIL

Fig. 46. CHOPPING PINS OF LAPPED DOVETAIL

Fig. 47. ARCOY DOVETAILER IN USE

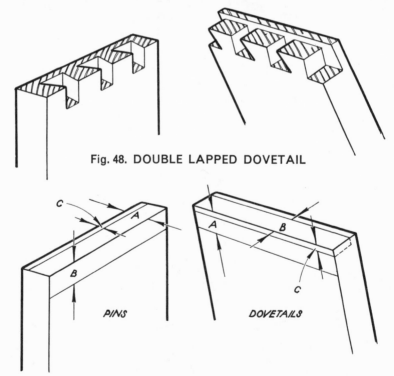

Fig. 48. DOUBLE LAPPED DOVETAIL

Fig. 49. GAUGING FOR DOUBLE LAPPED DOVETAIL

as in the through dovetail, except that the pins can only be partially sawn (as far as the diagonal). The rest has to be chopped with the chisel. Again chop down about $\frac{1}{16}$ in. from the gauge line, and split out the waste by a cut from the end. This will have to be done in several stages, as in Fig. 46. When nearly down another cut is made right on the gauge line. The sloping sides of the sockets will have to be chiselled in from the end, and a bevel-edged chisel will be invaluable. A narrow chisel or one sharpened at an angle will be needed to reach into the corners.

The lapped dovetail can also be cut with the electric router if the special attachment and bit is used, also with the Arcoy dovetailer which is used with an electric drill (Fig. 47). It can only be used for wood up to the limit of its width (about 9 in.). Sometimes the width is such that the spacing of dovetails

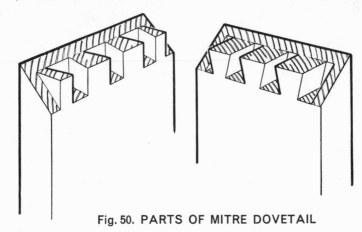

Fig. 50. PARTS OF MITRE DOVETAIL

is awkward, leaving part of a dovetail at one end, and then it is necessary to use the variable pitch attachment. Drawer dovetails are rather special and call for the arrangement in Chapter 6.

Double-lapped Dovetails
When there is an objection to the dovetails showing on either face, either the double-lap, or the mitre dovetail must be used. The former is similar to the lap-dovetail already dealt with but a lap is allowed on both pieces, one of them projecting as in Fig. 48, generally that with the dovetails. If, however, it is on the piece with the pins it is necessary to cut the latter first and mark the dovetails from it. The method of gauging the parts is shown in Fig. 49.

Secret Mitre Dovetail
In the mitre dovetail both parts have a projecting lap which is mitred, and the

73

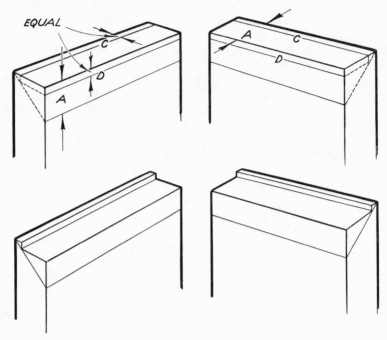

Fig. 51. GAUGING SECRET MITRE DOVETAIL

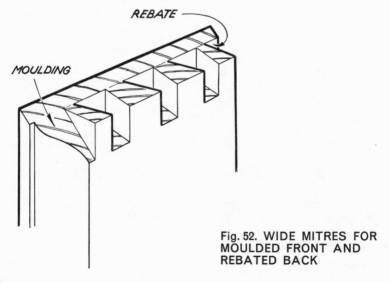

Fig. 52. WIDE MITRES FOR MOULDED FRONT AND REBATED BACK

front edge is mitred also as in Fig. 50. The pins must be cut first because it is impossible to mark the pins from the dovetails. Preliminary gauging is as in Fig. 51, and the pins are sawn and chopped in their entirety, but the mitres are not worked at this stage. By placing the piece to be dovetailed flat on the bench, and erecting that with the pins on it in the exact position, the joint shapes can be traced with the marking awl.

When sawing both pins and dovetails the saw will catch across the corner of the projecting lap, but this will not matter because the marks are removed later when the mitres are planed. To ensure that the slope is accurate a guiding block should be planed at 45 degrees, and cramped temporarily to the side of the wood, the corners coinciding as in Fig. 53. Thus in the finishing

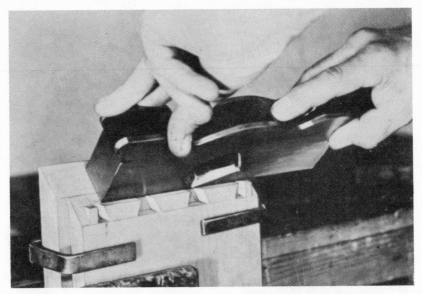

Fig. 53. PLANING MITRED LAP WITH SHOULDER PLANE

strokes the sole of the plane rests upon the bevel. The front and back mitres are sawn. It should be noted that when a moulding or wide chamfer has to be worked at the front edges the dovetails should be set in correspondingly, the amount depending upon the moulding depth. The same thing applies to the back when a rebate is needed. Fig. 52 shows the idea.

Mitres

Most mitres occur at the junction of pieces meeting at right angles. The mitre is therefore at 45 degrees. It should be realized at the outset that the angle of the mitre is always half that of the over-all angle (see Fig. 54). Consequently when pieces join at odd angles the mitre is not at 45 degrees. Thus if the over-all angle is 120 degrees the mitre angle is 60 degrees.

Fig. 54. MITRE LINE HALVES OVER-ALL ANGLE

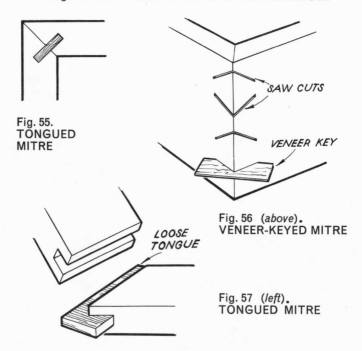

Fig. 55.
TONGUED
MITRE

SAW CUTS

VENEER KEY

LOOSE TONGUE

Fig. 56 (*above*).
VENEER-KEYED MITRE

Fig. 57 (*left*).
TONGUED MITRE

The parts may have to be mitred in either thickness (as in, say, a plinth) or in width as in a frame. The principle is the same, but the method of cutting or strengthening varies. When the mitring is in thickness the mitre may be quite plain, possibly nailed as well as glued, and with internal glue blocks rubbed in the angle. Generally a method of strengthening is needed, and this depends upon requirements. The strongest joint is the mitre dovetail (see page 73), but the expense is not always warranted, and a simpler alternative is the loose tongue, as in Fig. 55. Note that the grooves are towards the heel rather than the toe so that the tongue can be reasonably long without cutting across the wood unduly. Such a groove is awkward to cut by hand because the sloping grain is liable to result in the corner crumbling away. It is usually therefore confined to narrow pieces in which the grooves can be sawn and chiselled. If the electric router or spindle moulder is available there is no difficulty.

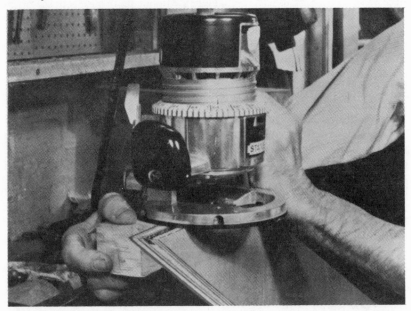

Fig. 58. CUTTING GROOVE ON MITRE WITH ELECTRIC ROUTER

When the surfaces are to be veneered or painted the mitre can be veneer-keyed as in Fig. 56. Saw cuts are made across the corner after the parts have been glued together, and little slips of veneer glued in the kerfs. Such a joint is suitable for small boxes, etc., which are later veneered.

When wood is mitred across the width the loose tongue is generally the best method of strengthening (Fig. 57). It may run right through or be stopped at one or both sides. It is more convenient to let it run right through (especially in handwork) if its appearance is not an objection. With relatively narrow pieces the grooves can be cut by part sawing and part chiselling to gauged lines, finishing off with a small hand-router to ensure the depth being equal throughout. For wider pieces the plough or grooving plane can be used, though this

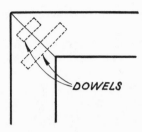

Fig. 59. DOWELLED MITRE

DOWELS

necessitates using the tool from the face side in one piece and from the reverse in the other owing to the sloping direction of the grain. This, in turn, requires that the wood is of equal thickness throughout. Assuming this to be the case there is no difficulty. Generally both pieces are of the same thickness, and then if the groove is centred the parts go together flush.

If, as sometimes happens, the groove has to be stopped at the outer corner the plough is used for as far as is practicable, and a special scratch stock substituted to finish off. Alternatively, the hand router with a fence fixed along it can be used, a narrow chisel or other cutter being used.

The electric router can be used, but, since there is usually a wide hole in the face plate, it is awkward to avoid dropping down too deeply. This can be overcome by fitting a special plastic face plate with a hole in it slightly bigger than the cutter, and fitting a deep wood block to act as a fence. This depth is helpful as it is a guide to holding the tool exactly square (see Fig. 58). In another, and possibly better way, the router can be reversed beneath a table fitted with a deep fence, and the wood passed across this.

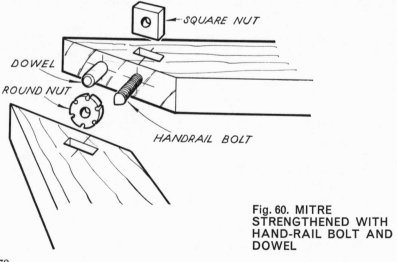

SQUARE NUT

DOWEL

ROUND NUT

HANDRAIL BOLT

Fig. 60. MITRE STRENGTHENED WITH HAND-RAIL BOLT AND DOWEL

An alternative is the use of dowels. At least two are needed to resist any twisting tendency. Their position can be marked with the gauge, and it should be noted that those towards the heel can be longer than the others (Fig. 59). For mitres subjected to much stress a stronger joint is that made with a handrail bolt, as in Fig. 60. This holds the parts together, and a dowel prevents any twisting. The position of the bolt at the mitre is squared round on to the rear, and an oblong slot chopped in line with it. In the one piece a square nut is slipped in and the bolt screwed into it. The free end of the bolt is passed into the hole in the other piece to engage with the circular nut passed into the slot. This circular nut is tightened with a special punch or, at a pinch, with the end of a screwdriver.

When the appearance of dowel ends at the outside does not matter, it is often an advantage to assemble the plain mitre and bore the dowel holes right through the joint after the glue has set.

JOINTS IN COMPOSITE BOARDS

Built-up boards invariably call for special type joints—and indeed of special forms of construction, details of which depend upon the particular kind of board. All of them are essentially panel materials, and, except in a few exceptional cases should not be used for framing parts. It follows, then, that nearly all the joints used are for joining parts at right angles to their thickness, as, for instance, in making a box or cabinet carcase. Exceptions are when it is necessary to fix a solid wood edging or lipping to conceal the thicknesses or to enable fittings, etc., to be added.

To an extent the type of joint depends upon whether the job has to be veneered and be polished, or whether it is to be painted. It should be realized at the outset that veneer does not take well over end grain, and, furthermore, any joints are liable to show through eventually to the surface. However, it is

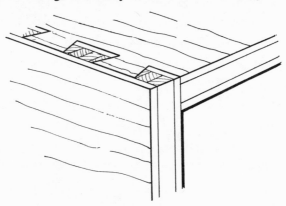

Fig. 61. LAPPED
DOVETAIL FOR
BLOCKBOARD

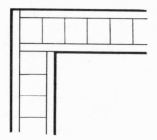

Fig. 62. SIMPLE
LAPPED JOINT

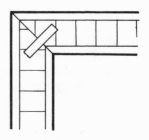

Fig. 63. TONGUED
MITRE

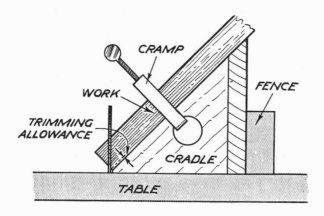

Fig. 64. CUTTING
MITRE ON
CIRCULAR SAW

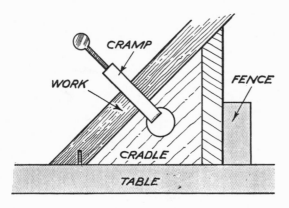

Fig. 65. GROOVE
OF MITRE CUT
ON CIRCULAR
SAW

largely a matter of considering each job on its merits. One other point fundamentally affecting the construction is that veneer should be laid on plywood or blockboard with its grain at right angles with that of the outer layers. Thus, if a long narrow door or table-top is to have the grain running lengthwise, the outer layers of the ply should run the short way. However, this is dealt with more fully in Chapter 7.

Plywood and blockboard can be dovetailed, but the members should not be fine as they would be liable to crumble. When only one surface of the job is normally seen the lap-dovetail is satisfactory as shown in Fig. 61. It could be applied to the corners of a cabinet if a separate top were fitted. In such a case solid wood rails would often be used rather than a plywood top, but the joint would be much the same. In another way the plain lapped joint in Fig. 62 could be used, this being glued and nailed. The grooved joint is of little value since the joint would be liable to fail along the layers of the ply or blockboard.

Another joint sometimes used when both surfaces must be free of visible joints, is the tongued mitre in Fig. 63. This, however, is suitable only for machine work, as it is awkward to work by hand except in small sizes owing to the short grain being liable to crumble.

There are several ways in which the grooves can be worked by machine. When the circular-saw is available this can be used for both sawing the mitre and cutting the groove. A special cradle is made up as in Fig. 64, the supports of which are at 45 degrees. The wood is cut off square first and the cradle then put in position. The set-up should be such that the saw just leaves a narrow uncut square at the end which just beds down on the table ($\frac{1}{32}$ in. is about right). To cut the groove the wood is reversed, as in Fig. 65, and the saw set to the cut of the groove depth.

Another method is to use the electric router. It is a help if the two pieces are placed face to face so that the machine has a bearing on both the sole and fence. It is a great help in holding the machine square. As there is usually a large gap in the sole the tool is liable to drop too far on to the wood at the start and end of the movement. This can be overcome by fitting a special sole plate (it can be of plastic material or thin plywood or metal) with a hole in it big enough only to allow the cutter to pass through. If preferred, the router can be placed upside down beneath a table and the work passed across it. In this case the cradle already mentioned for use with the saw can be used. One advantage of the router is that the groove can be stopped at either end.

The spindle moulder can be used equally well, of course—in fact the electric router when stationary beneath a table virtually becomes a spindle moulder.

3 Furniture Construction

THE METHOD OF making the parts of furniture may be conveniently divided under three headings: *framed*, as in doors, etc; *stool*, as in chairs and stools, cabinet stands, and so on; and *box*, such as carcases and drawers. The types are exemplified in Fig. 1.

Framed Construction

Here there are stiles (uprights) and rails (horizontals) joined together, preferably with mortise and tenon joints or dowels, with panels which fit in either grooves or rebates (Fig. 2). The panel is never glued, the reason being that it is free to shrink. A solid panel, if glued, would be liable to split in the event of shrinkage. The exact form of the joint depends upon the panel fitting and the details required, but usually it is one of those shown on pages 50–54 Sometimes several rails and muntins may be fitted.

In some cases four frames may be made up separately and jointed together afterwards with a tongue as shown at (A), Fig. 2, in which case it still remains

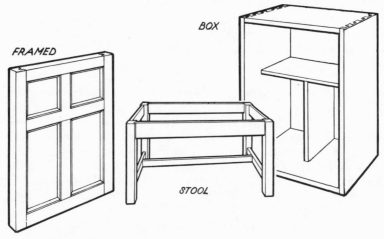

Fig. 1. THREE MAIN FORMS OF FURNITURE CONSTRUCTION

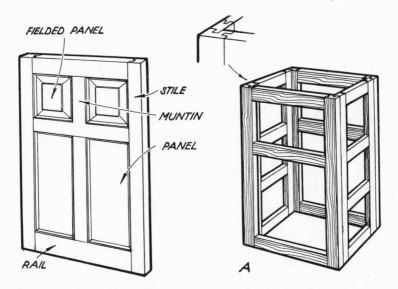

Fig. 2. FRAMED CONSTRUCTION SHOWING STILES AND RAILS
Sometimes a carcase is made in this way (A), consisting of four frames
fixed together

framed construction, and differs from stool construction in which there are
corner posts or squares into which both side and front rails are tenoned.

Sometimes table and similar tops are framed, the panel either fitting flush
or possibly recessed slightly to receive a covering of leather or baize. The
framing may be either tenoned or mitred.

Stool Construction
Items such as cabinet stands, stools, chairs, etc., come under the general
heading of stool construction. The legs are joined with a series of rails which
in the best work are tenoned into the legs. Sometimes stretchers are addition-
ally fitted. A typical arrangement is shown in Fig. 3. When the legs are of
fairly bold section the tenons can be central of the rails as at (A), but for a
slighter section it is better to offset them towards the outer side as they then
have maximum length (B). The ends can be either cut off at an angle in the
form of an open mitre, or halving can be cut as at (C). If the rails are set in
slightly from the face of the legs they must be cleaned up before assembling.

Stretchers
Stretchers may take various forms, some of which are shown in Fig. 4. When

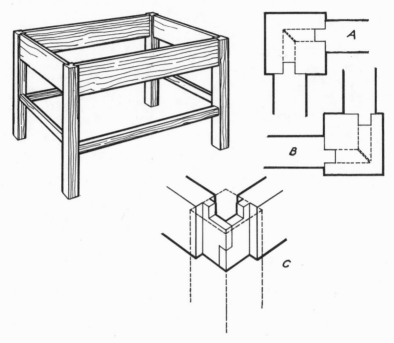

Fig. 3. TYPICAL STOOL OR STAND CONSTRUCTION
Variations of joints shown at A, B, and C

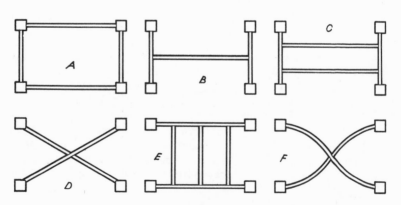

Fig. 4. VARIOUS STRETCHER ARRANGEMENTS

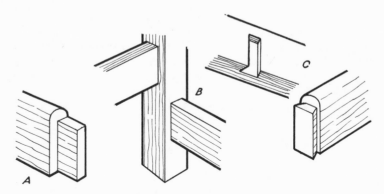

Fig. 5. JOINTS AND DETAILS OF STRETCHERS

the material is thin the tenons may be bare-faced as at (A), Fig. 5. Staggered rails (B) have an advantage in that the tenons can be of maximum length since they do not interfere with each other, and the leg is not weakened by the adjoining mortises. Sometimes either the end or the long stretchers are not fitted directly to the legs, but are joined to the other stretchers as at (B, C, and E), Fig. 4. The best joint in this case is the slot-dovetail stopped at the top so that it does not show (C), Fig. 5.

A type of stand that has become popular in recent years is that in Fig. 6. As the legs stand in at the end they are joined by a form of bridle joint (X). The cross-rails may either enter the legs (A), in which case they are tenoned in, or they may join the long rails (B) with either stub tenons (C) or with a slot-dovetail (D).

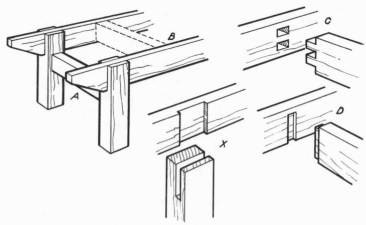

Fig. 6. LEGS SET IN FROM RAIL ENDS

85

Sometimes the legs are set at a slight angle and either the shoulders of the rails have to be cut at a corresponding angle, or the tops of the legs tapered. When the stand is quite low the method in Fig. 7 is sometimes followed, this having the advantage of enabling square shoulders to be cut. On the other hand, it involves the use of more material.

When the legs slope in front elevation only, the front and back shoulders are cut an an angle, and the others made square. Sometimes the legs splay in

Fig. 7. SLOPING LEG CUT FROM LARGE BLOCK

both directions and then theoretically the shoulders are at a compound angle in that they slope in plan as well as elevation. In practice, however, unless the slope is really pronounced, the plan angle can be ignored since it is so slight that the difference is nothing more than a thin shaving will correct.

Items such as chairs call for angled joints because the seat is wider at front than back. In the best way the mortises are made to slope and the tenons cut square because the grain of the tenons is thus parallel with that of the rails; whereas it runs at an angle when the mortises are cut in square. However, in the trade the latter is sometimes followed because it involves using a special cradle to hold the wood at an angle when mortising.

Dowels are widely used in the trade for all forms of stand construction, though they are not so satisfactory as the mortise and tenon joint. It is always advisable to fit up some special form of guide, whether machine or hand methods are used, because dowels rely upon accurate fitting for their strength.

Box Construction

This includes all box-like items such as cabinet carcases consisting of two ends, top, bottom, and back; drawers; and so on. The corners are jointed in various ways according to requirements, some being shown in Fig. 8. For a cabinet in which there is a separate top the lapped dovetail (A) is widely used as it is entirely concealed at the sides. There may be a solid false top, or there may be two rails with angle braces as shown by the dotted lines.

A growing tendency today is to use frankly exposed joints, and if they are well cut they certainly have a decorative value. They may be straightforward dovetails with equal spacing of tails and pins, or they may have the decorative arrangement shown at (B). There is no advantage so far as strength is concerned.

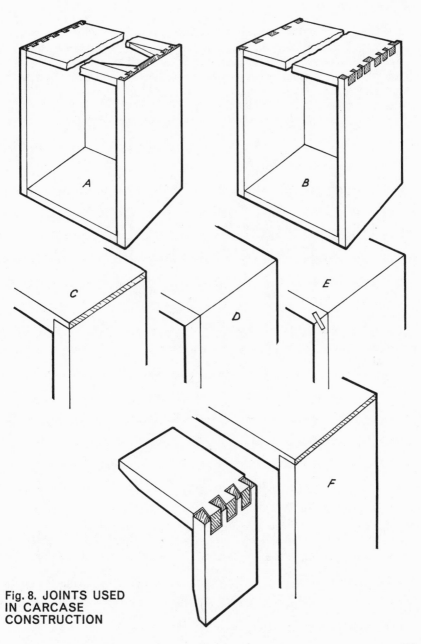

Fig. 8. JOINTS USED
IN CARCASE
CONSTRUCTION

Another method of half-concealing the joint is to use the double-lapped dovetail (C) which shows merely as a narrow line of end grain at the side. For complete concealment the mitre dovetail (D) is used. A rather simpler mitre joint is that at (E) in which the plain mitre is grooved to receive a tongue. It is ideal when machinery is available, but is not easy to cut by hand owing to the tendency of the short grain to crumble. The grooves could be stopped at the front when the spindle moulder or router is available.

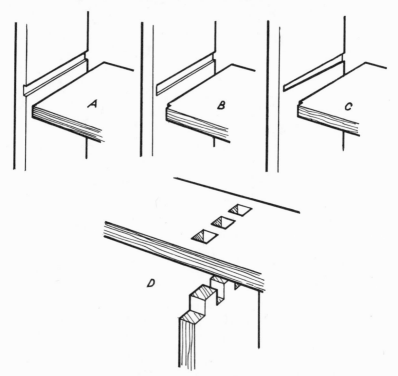

Fig. 9. METHODS OF FIXING SHELVES AND PARTITIONS

In some circumstances the method at (F) has an advantage. A quite simple joint such as a plain lap or mitre can be cut and strengthened with dovetailed brackets screwed on at the inside. It is advisable to cut the ends of both pins and tails slightly short so that if the wood shrinks the ends are not left projecting. In any case the extreme corner is removed. If one of the manu-factured boards is used for the main carcase a plain square can be glued in the angle and screwed in both directions. This should not be done in the case of solid wood as it resists shrinkage.

Whatever the method used it is necessary to make allowance at the back for any rebate that may be needed to receive the back, and possibly at the front for any moulded edge. When there is a separate top, the false or under-top usually stands in by the rebate depth, the back fitting behind it. This invariably happens at the bottom in any case. When there is no separate top the rebate has to be continued along the top as well as at the sides.

Sometimes shelves or partitions have to be built in, and one of the methods in Fig. 9 is usual. The simplest is the plain housing (A) which necessarily shows at the front. By stopping the housing (B) a neater job is produced. A rather stronger joint is the bare-faced dovetail housing (C), also stopped at the front. Note that it tapers from back to front, the advantage being that the joint is quite loose until the shelf is nearly home. It makes fitting much simpler.

A vertical partition can be strongly held by the pinned joint (D). Clearly it is practicable only in positions where it is later concealed, or when used to give a decorative effect. It is usually wedged at the outside afterwards, either diagonally or at each side across the grain.

4 Marking Out

THIS MAY BE conveniently divided up under two headings; the preliminary marking out of wood in the rough to be sawn to size; and the final marking out of the pieces for joint cutting, rebating, grooving, and so on.

Preliminary Marking

This is done in pencil, and allowance for working has to be made. Cutting lists are often provided giving this allowance, which varies with the size of the job, but is usually in the region of $\frac{1}{2}$ in. in length, and $\frac{1}{8}$ in. to $\frac{1}{4}$ in. in width. Thicknesses are usually net—at any rate when machine-planed timber is used, which is usual nowadays. The special purpose of the particular item has to be considered, however. For instance, stiles which have to be mortised at the ends should have about $\frac{1}{2}$ in. waste at each end to avoid the tendency of the short grain to split when mortising. Parts to be tenoned, however, need little or no allowance. Size affects the width because slight curvature in a short piece can be taken out with two or three shavings, whereas

Fig. 1. MARKING PARALLEL LINES WITH RULE AND FINGER

the same degree of curvature in a long piece would need considerably more planing to correct it.

For hand-working all lines have to be pencilled in, either a straight-edge and square being used, or if there is a straight edge to the wood the rule and finger gauge can be used (as in Fig. 1). In machine work it is always quicker to make one edge straight first because it is then only a matter of setting the ripping fence to the width required, any number of pieces being then cut out without marking the timber at all.

Shaped members can frequently be marked one inside the other so reducing waste (Fig. 2). In all this preliminary marking the positions of the parts should be considered, the best grain being retained for the show parts. Straightness of grain should also be considered, especially in narrow parts such as rails which might be seriously reduced in strength with unsuitable grain.

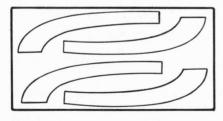

Fig. 2. ECONOMICAL MARKING OUT OF SHAPES

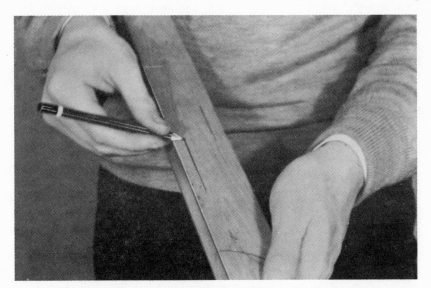

Fig. 3. PENCIL AND FINGER GAUGE FOR MARKING

Another point to be considered is that of cost. Narrow boards are cheaper per foot super than wide ones, and it is therefore advantageous to use up narrow stuff for rails, etc., rather than to cut up a wide board.

Close Marking

Final marking of parts to finished size and setting out of joints should be done whenever possible with marking knife or chisel, or with the gauge. Thus, all widths and thicknesses should be gauged once the face sides and edges have been made true. Halvings, tenons, dovetails, etc., are also gauged, and shoulders and similar parts cut in with knife or chisel, the square being used. The only exception is in such details as chamfers, certain mouldings, mortises, etc., in which cut-in lines would show as a blemish. Thus mortise lengths are squared across with pencil, and chamfers marked by the finger gauge method (Fig. 3), or by means of a notched block as in Fig. 4. A sharp pencil is held against the end of the wood, and the latter drawn along.

When more than one item has to be marked identically, as in the case of rails, they should be cramped together temporarily with their face edges uppermost, and the marks squared across all, as in Fig. 5. They are then separated and the lines squared around each individually. When this is being done the butt of the square should rest against either the face side or the face edge as this ensures that the lines meet.

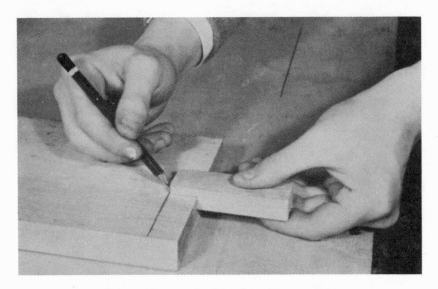

Fig. 4. MARKING WITH NOTCHED BLOCK.

When only two or three parts are being marked in this way there is no difficulty, but when a large number has to be marked there is the possibility of inaccuracy due to the wood being slightly out of truth. A slightly different length might be registered at the far side. It is therefore desirable to square the lines across first with a sharp pencil and measure to see whether their distance apart is the same at the back as at the front (see Fig. 6). If there is a difference it should be divided equally at the far side and a nick made with the corner of the knife at both near and far sides. The base of the square can then be made level with these marks by sliding it up to the knife held in each nick in turn.

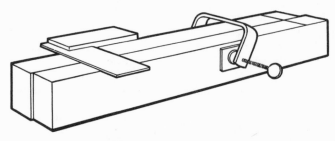

Fig. 5. MARKING A PAIR OF RAILS

Incidentally, when squaring around the sides and edges of rails it is always a help to place the knife or chisel at the corner of the mark previously made, and slide the square up to it. This ensures alignment and saves a good deal of time.

Dovetailed joints are usually gauged in, and when the mark has to be made across the grain the cutting gauge should be used (the marking gauge would scratch). Many object to this, especially in show work, in that it makes an unsightly mark across the root of the dovetail. However, it is possible to get around it by gauging lightly. The sides of the dovetail are then sawn, after which the marks at the intervening spaces can be deepened. The advantage of

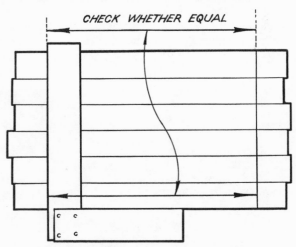

Fig. 6. MARKING SEVERAL MEMBERS

a deep cut is that it enables a sloping notch to be cut at the waste side, the chisel fitting in this for the final cut.

Whenever practicable all marking with the square is done with the butt against either the face side or face edge, but, like most rules, there are exceptions. For instance, in some shaped work there may be no option, and the only safeguard then is to work accurately, making sure that the back edges are straight, square, and parallel with the front.

5 Truing and Cleaning up

WOOD CAN BE obtained straight from the saw, or it may be ready planed. In the latter case, except for checking that surfaces and edges are true, and correcting if necessary, the parts can be sawn out straightway. If a circular saw is available the straight edge of the wood is run along the ripping fence. When a large machine planer can be used the board as a whole can be planed

Fig. 1. CLEANING UP FRAMEWORK WITH PLANE

and thicknessed and the individual parts cut out. It may be, however, that only a narrow machine is available—say 4 in., and in this case the parts are cut out first and planed afterwards. First the one surface of each part is taken over the machine, followed by one edge. Thicknessing follows, either the thicknessing machine or the thicknessing attachment being used. Fig. 7 on page 17 is a diagram showing this. Its action and method of use is described in Chapter 1. When the wood is sufficiently thick, say 1 in. or more, and is not too wide, it can be brought to width in the same way. Generally two parts can be passed through together.

In the case of hand-work the general procedure is much the same. It invariably pays to surface and thickness a board and then cut out the individual parts. One edge of each is made straight and square with the trying plane, and the other gauged parallel and planed to width. Marking out follows, after which the joints can be cut, and any detail worked.

Cleaning up

This is usually the last process because it is essential to avoid risk of the wood being marked. It does to an extent depend upon circumstances, however. Some parts must be cleaned up before assembling because it would be awkward or impossible to clean them afterwards. Others must be dealt with afterwards because they involve levelling operations.

Given a good up-to-date machine planer in good condition items such as tops and panels need only be passed through a sander after being planed. For cabinet work to be polished, however, the finish given by the small machine is not good enough. In the nature of things the rotating cutters leave a series of marks across the grain, the distance between them depending upon the number of cutters in the block, the speed of the block, and the rate at which the wood is passed across the cutters. If the cutters are dull the result is a series of hammer blows on the wood causing the grain to be compressed, and if later the wood is stained and polished the stresses are released causing a series of unsightly marks across the grain of the wood. If a cutter is gashed it will leave a track along the grain, and, although it may be sanded out, it will reappear when any stain or polish is applied.

Hand Planing

For these reasons it is best to regard a machine-planer as a means of truing the wood, and to clean up by hand. This involves setting the smoothing plane fine with the back iron close up the edge and with the mouth as fine as possible. In the case of difficult woods it is an advantage to use a high pitched plane as it has more of a scraping than a cutting action. Some men get over the problem by having a special cutter for such work, the edge being backed off which has the same effect as raising the pitch. It results in greater resistance, and should be used in special cases only. Furthermore, it involves the use of a specially shaped back iron.

Previous truing should, of course, have made the wood straight and flat, but minor details such as tears (pronounced 'tares') still remain, and these have to be taken out in the cleaning up. It is often a help to pass the hand lightly across the surface as any waves can thereby be detected easily. Some men prefer to sharpen the plane cutter straight with the corners taken off. The writer prefers to make it *slightly* rounded. Every part should be gone over, after which the scraper is used.

The purpose of this is twofold: it removes plane marks, and takes out any tears that even the finely set plane makes. Woods vary tremendously in their ease of cleaning up. With some the only need of scraping is that of removing plane marks: others tear out locally no matter which way they are planed. In such cases it sometimes pays to scrape first in one direction then the other. Alternatively, it may be necessary to scrape local tears in the direction best suited to them. Some of the worst woods are the softer but woollier hardwoods in which the grain lifts out as strings. A sharp scraper and a lot of patience is the only answer. The method of sharpening the scraper is given in page 35.

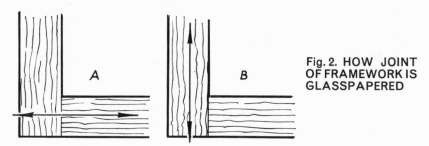

Fig. 2. HOW JOINT OF FRAMEWORK IS GLASSPAPERED

Glasspapering is the final process, and for the general run of woods Middle 2 followed by 1½ or 1 are needed. A cork glasspaper rubber should always be used as it is only by this means that the high parts are levelled. It is worked always in the direction of the grain. An exception, however, is that of such woods as burr walnut which have no grain direction and these should be finished with No. 0 paper used with a circular motion.

When cleaning such parts as door frames special precautions have to be taken as the tools cannot always be used in the direction of the grain, and at all cost it is necessary to avoid splintering out edges and corners. Generally it is best to use a slicing action as in Fig. 1. The important thing to avoid is running the plane outwardly across an edge whether it be the outer or the inner edge of the frame. The plane must be set fine, and if used so that it slices the wood it is possible to avoid tearing out. The scraper follows, and this again is used at an angle because it is inevitable that in parts it will be working across the grain.

Glasspapering follows, first Middle 2 then 1½ or 1, and this is held over the cork rubber and used on the rails first, as at (A), Fig. 2, being taken right across the shoulders. It will, of course, make marks on the stile at right

Fig. 3. USE OF
THE
ORBITAL
SANDER
FOR
CLEANING
UP

angles with the grain, but these marks are taken out when the glasspaper is used *with* the grain along the stiles (B). Care must be taken not to allow the rubber to stray across the shoulders of the rails. Finish in both directions with the Middle 2 first, then with the finer grade.

Glasspapering

The rule about glasspapering always in the direction of the grain cannot always be followed. For instance, when a frieze or similar rail is veneered across the grain it is not practicable to take the glasspaper across the rail, especially when it is narrow, and the only plan is to use nothing coarser than No. $1\frac{1}{2}$ and finish off with o. Much the same applies to panels with built-up designs in veneer—halved, quartered, or cross-banded. The only plan is to work in one direction only using fine paper.

Many men nowadays use a power-sander. In the trade the belt-sander is widely used for panels but it is a large machine, and most people now use the portable sander (Fig. 3). A type which has come in for wide use is the orbital type in which the pad moves in a series of small circles. It does not revolve in the ordinary sense of the word, and the best way of describing the movement is to think of a pencil dot made on the pad. This moves in a small circle when the sander is switched on. It thus makes a series of small circular scratches on the surface, which however are so small that they cannot be detected. The machine can thus be used for all flat surfaces, and is of particular advantage for built-up veneer designs, curly grained woods such as burr walnut, and for work involving joints such as door frames. One point to realize, however, is that the result of glasspapering across the grain is to make the wood more absorbent of stain. Consequently, if some parts of a job are sanded with the grain in the ordinary way, and some finished with the orbital sander, the latter will be slightly darker when stained.

In all sanding the important thing is to avoid dubbing over edges and corners. Thus as the glasspaper cork reaches the far end of a panel the pressure should be over the part left on the panel.

Mouldings call for the use of special wood rubbers shaped to a reverse of

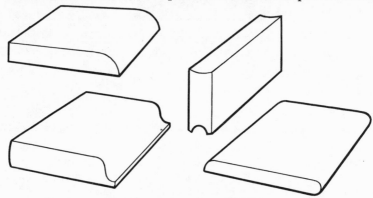

Fig. 4. GLASSPAPER RUBBERS FOR MOULDINGS

the moulding. Over the years one accumulates a number of such rubbers, rounds and hollows of varying curvations, ogees, and so on (Fig. 4). Do not attempt to finish the entire section of a large moulding in one operation; rather deal with each member in turn as in Fig. 5. (For cleaning up veneer work see Chapter 7.)

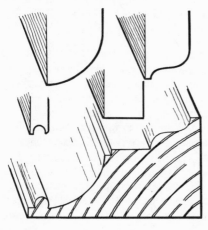

Fig. 5. RUBBERS NEEDED FOR GLASSPAPERING A LARGE MOULDING

6 Drawer and Door Making

IN THE BEST way drawers are still made with hand-cut dovetails. There is no machine which will cut the fine neat dovetails required. However, the machine dovetailer *can* be used, and there are various alternative simpler methods, all of which we discuss in this chapter.

Hand Dovetailing

Fig. 1 shows the setting out of the joints. The bottom is contained in grooved slips glued to the sides (three patterns of slips are given). As the front is thick it can be grooved to receive the bottom, and, since this groove has to run right through, it is essential for the lowest dovetail to include it. Otherwise it will show as a gap at the outside. At the rear the bottom has to slide in along the grooved slips, and the back has therefore to stand immediately above the bottom. Consequently the bottom square edge of the back runs right through, forming a bare-faced dovetail.

The benefit of the use of grooved bottom slips is that it avoids weakening the sides which would otherwise have to be grooved, and increases the bearing

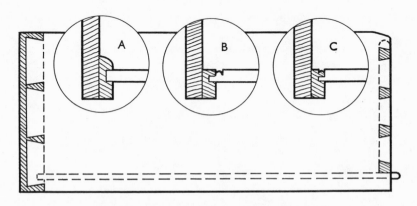

Fig. 1. DRAWER DOVETAILS AND SECTIONS OF SLIPS

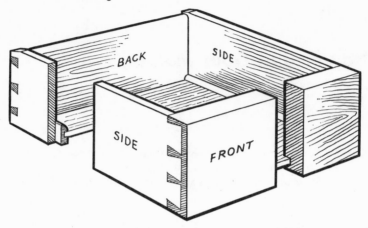

Fig. 2. CUT-AWAY VIEW OF DRAWER

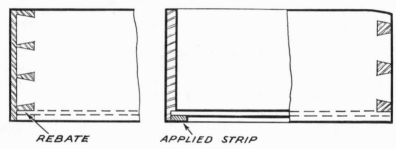

REBATE   *APPLIED STRIP*

Fig. 3. DOVETAILS OF SMALL DRAWER

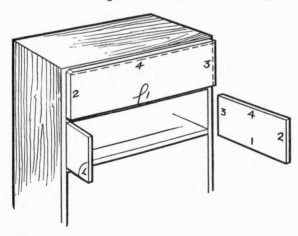

Fig. 4. FITTING
PARTS OF
DRAWER

surface, so reducing wear. There are exceptions to this general plan, particularly in small drawers in which the bottom is rebated in, and the arrangement here is shown in Fig. 3. Note that the rebate is $\frac{1}{16}$ in. to $\frac{1}{8}$ in. deeper than the thickness of the bottom, and thicknessing slips are glued in. These keep the bottom from scraping, and increase the bearing surface.

Making a Dovetailed Drawer

First fit the front to make a tight fit in its opening. Plane the bottom edge straight and trim one end a close fit against the opening. The other end is planed, again to fit closely, and finally the top edge (Fig. 4). It is a help if the edges are taken off slightly at an angle so that, although the inner face just passes in, the front face stands out. The angle should be no more than a fine shaving thickness.

The back is treated similarly, but the ends are trimmed on the shooting board so that they just fit in the space. The width is far less, of course, because the lower edge stands above the bottom, and the top one stands down so that it does not scrape (see Fig. 1).

When preparing the sides plane the bottom edge straight and make front and back edges square with it. Again the shooting board is the most convenient way of planing. Mark the front lower corner (R or L) as shown in Fig. 4, so that the position can be recognized, and finally trim the top edge so that the side makes a fairly tight fit when tried in position. Incidentally when calculating the length remember to deduct the lap allowed at the front.

The dovetails can now be set out and sawn. The pins between the tails run nearly to a point. If it is decided to transfer the shape to the pins by drawing the saw through the kerfs this should now be done before chiselling away the waste. Otherwise the latter is done first and the marks transferred with a marking awl.

Before assembling, groove the front to receive the bottom, and clean up all inner surfaces. Also round over the top edge of the back. Place a flat block over the joints when knocking home as otherwise the wood may be bruised, and in any case it might split owing to the localized blow. Test for squareness, and leave to set.

Fitting

To avoid racking the drawer, fix a piece of wood to overhang the edge of the bench and rest the drawer on this. Long drawers would need two supports, as in Fig. 5. Test frequently into the carcase, and do not remove shavings until it is obvious where the drawer is tight. It is usual to take off the back corners at a slight angle so that the movement is eased. Slide the bottom in from the back and fix with screws. Nowadays plywood or hardboard is used, and with these there is no shrinkage problem. In the case of solid wood, the back edge

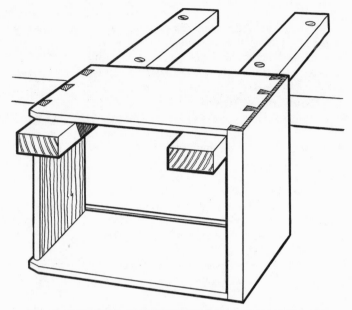

Fig. 5. HOLDING DRAWER WHILST CLEANING UP

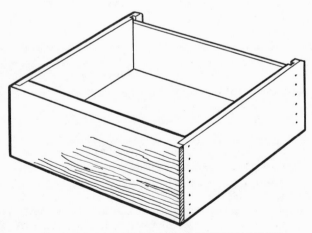

Fig. 6. SIMPLE FORM OF CONSTRUCTION

should be allowed to project so that in the event of shrinkage the whole bottom can be pushed forward and fixed at the back through fresh screw holes. After polishing has been completed the moving parts can be lubricated with candle grease rubbed on cold.

Those who have a machine dovetailing device may prefer to use this. Generally it is necessary to use the multi-pitch type as otherwise the dovetails may not space out suitably. This will cut the front-lapped dovetails, but these are unsuitable for the back, and the usual plan is to fit this in grooves cut across the sides as in Fig. 6. Incidentally it is generally advisable to space the dovetails from the bottom because then the groove in the front to hold the bottom is contained within the bottom dovetail.

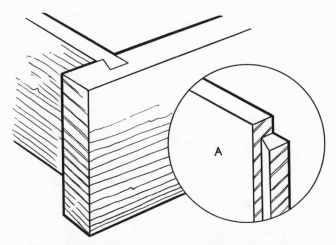

Fig. 7. SLOT-DOVETAIL FOR DRAWER FRONT

A cheap alternative construction is that in Fig. 6 in which the front is rebated to hold the sides which are glued and nailed, and the back fitted in grooves. It is a method often used for kitchen cabinets and similar pieces. In this case, since the sides are fairly thick, they can be grooved to hold the bottom. The back stands up above the latter.

Sometimes the sides cannot be fitted at the ends of the front, but have to be set in. The bare-faced slot dovetail is then used (Fig. 7). This can either run right through or be stopped short of the top edge, as at (A). The latter makes the neater job.

A method of drawer fitting that was popular centuries ago and which shows signs of coming into fashion again was that in which broad grooves were cut in the centre of the sides to engage central runners (Fig. 8). It necessitates

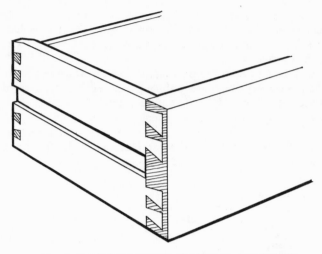

Fig. 8. DRAWER WITH CENTRAL RUNNERS

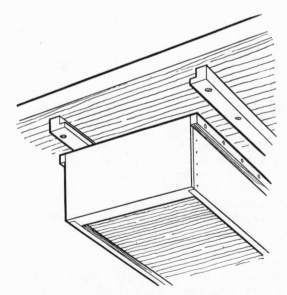

Fig. 9. SUSPENDED DRAWER

having fairly thick sides to enable the grooves to be worked, and has the advantage that no stops are needed as the front strikes against the bearers. It is a method that can be used only when the sides are thick enough to permit the grooving, and even then the bearing surface is limited.

Occasionally a drawer has to be carried immediately beneath a top, there being no supporting sides or lower rail. Fillets are fixed to the top of the drawer sides and rebated runners screwed beneath the top as in Fig. 9.

DOORS

For furniture these are of two general kinds; flush and framed. The former are generally of veneered plywood or blockboard, though veneering is not necessary on a job to be painted.

Flush Doors

As a rule lipping is necessary to hide the layers at the edges, but may also be required to give a fixing for fittings (screws do not hold well when driven into the edge of plywood). In this case the lipping has to be wider. Methods of

A   B

Fig. 10. LIPPINGS FOR FLUSH DOORS

lipping are given in Fig. 10. That shown at (A) is satisfactory but is awkward to work by hand. If a portable electric router is available it is easily made. It can be added either before or after veneering. The latter has the advantage of protecting the edge of the veneer, which is always the most vulnerable part, but it necessarily shows, of course. Wider lippings are better fixed with a loose tongue as at (B). If it is still desired to protect the veneer edge a separate tongue can be added as shown.

Grain Direction

At the outset it should be realized that the grain of the veneer should, if possible, be at right angles with that of the outer layer of the ply as at (A), Fig. 11. Otherwise there is danger of fine hair cracks opening up. It is satisfactory if the veneer runs at an angle, however, as for instance if the veneer is quartered as at (B). Both sides of the panel should be veneered to avoid its being pulled hollow. Further details of this are given in the chapter on veneering.

When cutting out the material for the main panel it is obviously necessary to allow for the edging to be added. If it is to be added after veneering it should only be necessary to take off a skim for final trimming as otherwise the edging will show unevenly. To ensure a minimum of trimming the panel should be planed to a good fit against the actual carcase. The order is shown in Fig. 12. Plane the bottom edge so that both it and the hingeing edge agree with the carcase. This may sound obvious, but if the latter should be not quite square the door must agree with it. Now cut the length equal to the opening height less the combined thickness of the two lippings with just a

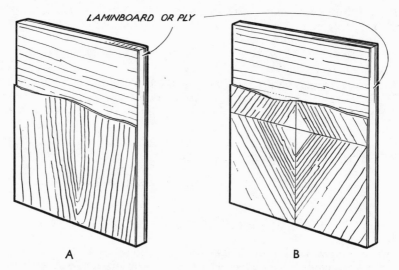

LAMINBOARD OR PLY

A   B

Fig. 11. GRAIN DIRECTION OF VENEER FOR PLY OR LAMIN BOARD

trifle fullness. Do the same with the width, then raise the panel to the top and trim, if necessary, to see that it aligns with the carcase top. In width the panel should show a parallel gap from top to bottom.

When a piece of really sound, well-seasoned wood is available this can sometimes be used as a flush door as it is, especially when only a narrow door is needed. A wider one is more difficult and jointing will probably be needed. One method which was often used by cabinet-makers in the past was to cut straight-grained strips about 2 in. wide and glue them together with the heart sides alternating out and in. After levelling and fitting the whole was veneered both sides. In first class work counter-veneering gave a really reliable result (Fig. 13).

Another form of flush door is made with relatively thin plywood fixed to

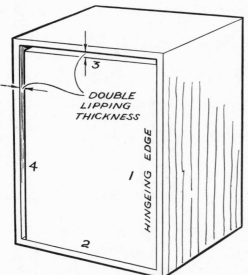

Fig. 12. **ALLOWANCE FOR LIPPING IN FLUSH DOOR**

DOUBLE LIPPING THICKNESS

HINGEING EDGE

Fig. 13 (*right*).   FLUSH DOOR WITH SOLID STRIPS FOR GROUNDWORK. BEST WORK IS COUNTER-VENEERED

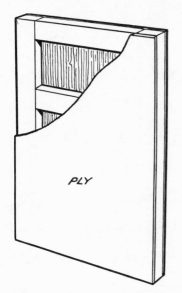

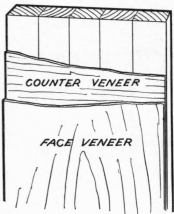

COUNTER VENEER

FACE VENEER

PLY

Fig. 14. ALTERNATIVE CONSTRUCTION

Fig. 15. SQUARE-EDGED FRAME WITH APPLIED MOULDINGS

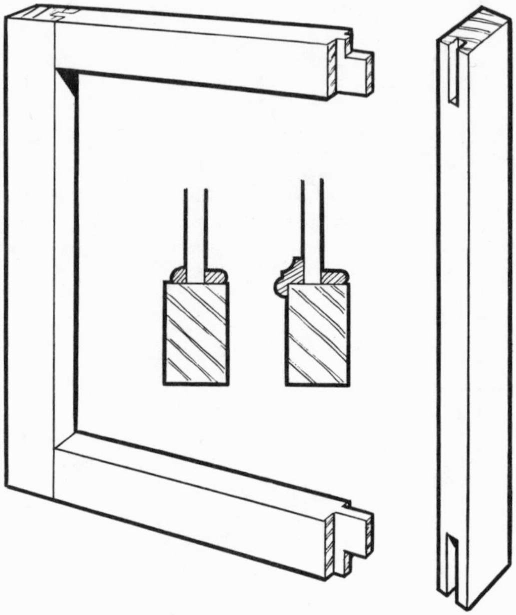

Fig. 16 (*below*).
MOULDED AND REBATED FRAMEWORK

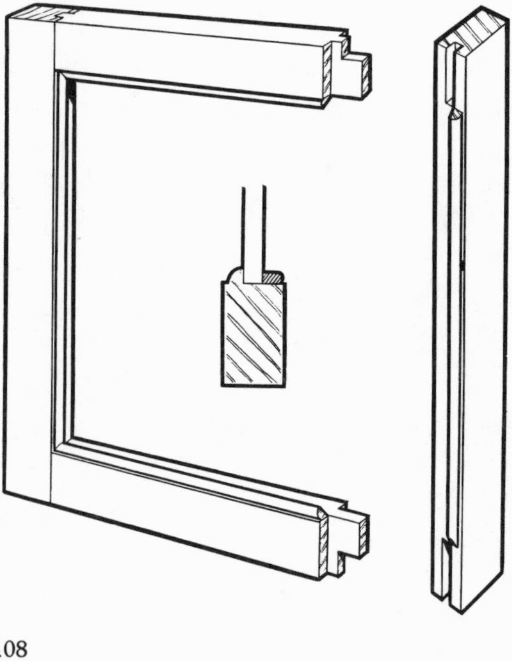

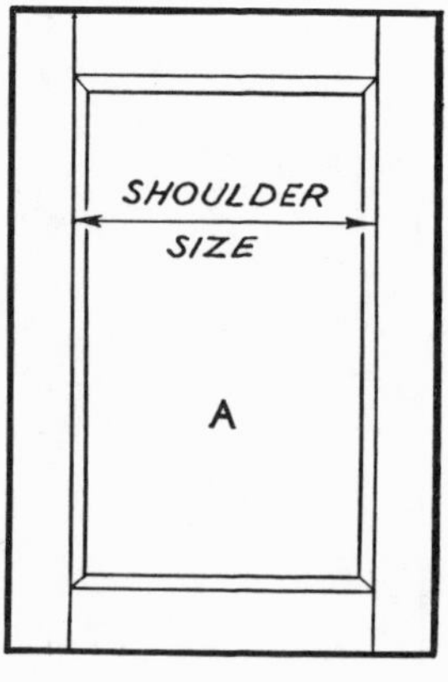

SHOULDER
SIZE

A

a framework as in Fig. 14. Usually the ply is veneered, and in good quality work a ply panel is fitted to each side of the frame work. The same idea is widely used in light doors for items such as kitchen fitments to be painted.

A point to note is that if the door is of any size it is advisable to fit one or more intermediate rails as otherwise the panel may tend to sag in the middle.

Framed Doors

There are many variations of this type. The panel usually fits in a rebate where it is held with a bead mitred round. Grooved-in panels are seldom used as the panel has to be inserted during assembly, and it is awkward to polish afterwards. The best joint is the mortise and tenon, of which there are many variations which depend upon the detail of the door. The example in Fig. 15 show the joints for the square-edged frame with applied moulding. Sometimes dowels are used, but they are not so reliable as the mortise and tenon.

Other types of doors with rebated and moulded framework, grooved in panel, and rebated frame are given in Figs. 16, 17, and 18.

The procedure is much the same in all, except that in the type with panel rebate and stuck moulding (Fig. 16) the shoulder length is taken to the rebate depth which is usually level with the bottom of the moulding (see A). The

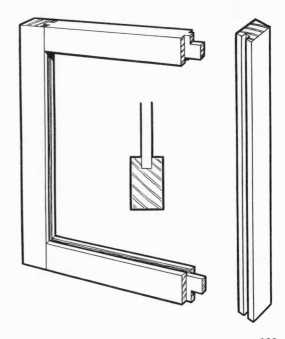

Fig. 17. **DOOR WITH GROOVED-IN PANEL**

reason, of course, is that the moulding of the stiles has to be cut back locally opposite the joint, hence the increased shoulder length.

Marking Out

To mark the stiles one of the pieces is placed against the carcase, as in Fig. 19, and the length marked with pencil. The two are then placed together with the edges uppermost and the marks squared across both with about $\frac{1}{16}$ in. added for trimming (it is less than this for a small door). In all door work an extra length of about 1 in. is always allowed over the finished size because

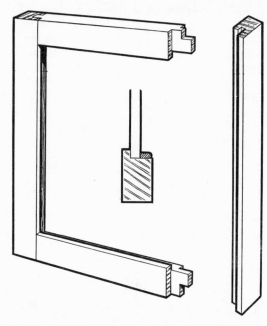

Fig. 18. DOOR WITH REBATED-IN PANEL

there would otherwise be liability for the wood to split. Whilst the two parts are still held together the over-all rail width is squared in; also the set-in of the haunch and the groove or rebate depth. Fig. 19 shows the idea.

Rail length follows, and here the simplest way is to place the two stiles in the carcase, and obtain the shoulder length by direct marking as in Fig. 20. This is marked in pencil and again about $\frac{1}{16}$ in. added when the rails are fixed together and the marks squared across with chisel or knife. The parts are then separated and the marks squared round each rail individually. In the case of a moulded and rebated door the shoulder length is increased by the rebate depth at each end as already mentioned. Here the length is obtained by gauging the rebate lines on the stiles, and marking to these gauge lines.

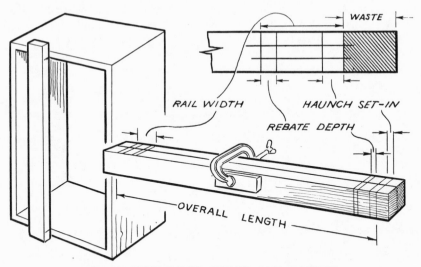

Fig. 19. HOW DOOR STILES ARE MARKED

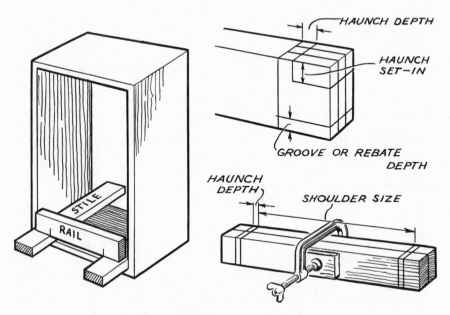

Fig. 20. MARKING OUT DOOR RAILS

A point to note is that, in the case of tenons to be machine-sawn, both tenons must be of exactly the same length because the end of the rail is placed on the saw table and the saw thus cuts up an equal amount in every case. Consequently the rail must be placed exactly centrally when marking.

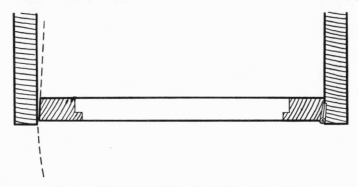

Fig. 21. WHY CLOSING EDGE IS AT ANGLE

This is not specially important in hand work as sawing can cease when the shoulder line is reached.

Notes on sawing tenons are given in Chapter 2. Do not saw the shoulders until after rebating (first) and moulding (second) have been completed. Mortising is the first operation on the stiles, followed again by rebating and moulding.

The door having been assembled, fitting can follow. Plane the hingeing edge true, and trim the bottom to a close fit with the carcase. Follow with the top edge, and finally the closing edge. It should be noted that if much has to be taken from the width both stiles should be planed equally, otherwise the difference in width will become obvious. For a cabinet door clearance is about the thickness of brown paper, though it does to an extent depend upon the size of the door. Finally the closing edge should be at a slight angle, as in Fig. 21, as otherwise it will bind when opened.

Large Doors

Construction depends upon the purpose of the door and the effect required. The simplest form is that used for sheds and is known as the ledged and braced door (Fig. 22). It consists of a series of tongued and grooved boards held together with cross-pieces or ledges with sloping braces to prevent sagging. The fixing nails pass through the tongued boards and the ledges and are clenched over. It is advisable to fix the ledges with two or three temporary

Fig. 22. LEDGED AND BRACED
DOOR

Fig. 23 (*below*). FRAMED AND
BRACED DOOR

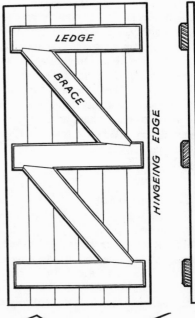

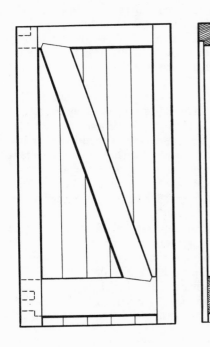

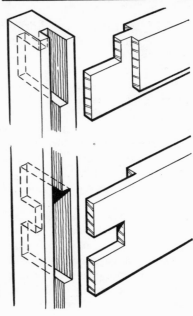

113

nails, before turning the whole over and nailing from the front. In the best way the braces are let into notches cut in the braces as shown. Remember that the latter always slope downward towards the hingeing side.

A better type of door is framed and braced (Fig. 23). Stiles and top rail are of equal thickness, but the bottom rail (and mid-rail if there is one) is thinner by the thickness of the tongued and grooved boarding which passes in front of it. The stiles and top rail are usually rebated to receive the boarding.

Room and street doors are either framed or flush. It is seldom that one bothers to make them as they are available ready-made in a variety of sizes and designs. When fitting, an allowance should be made all round for the thickness of the paint. This is usually reckoned as the thickness of a shilling piece.

Tambour Doors

These can be used in positions where ordinary hingeing would cause a door to foul some other part, though they frequently are used purely as a matter of preference. It is, however, at the sacrifice of a certain amount of space in the interior since the door has to slide in at the side and often around the back as well. Grooves in the top and bottom guide the tambour, and frequently, though not invariably, the ends of the tambour are shouldered, the advantage being that the grooves are entirely concealed, regardless of the section of the tambours.

The last-named may be flat or moulded. In the first case the pieces may be cut from a single board and assembled in the same order. If the joints are carefully made it is impossible to detect the fact that the pieces are separate and not a single panel. Alternatively, different woods are sometimes used alternately. In the case of moulded tambours the pieces may consist of a separate mould each, or, if the section is narrow, two moulds may be worked in each piece. When veneer is used it is desirable to veneer both sides as otherwise the parts may tend to bow. The parts being cut and trimmed to make close joints, they are laid out flat on a board which has a shallow fence at each side so that the ends are in alignment, as in Fig. 24. They are pressed close together and held by a strip of wood nailed at the end. Pressure should not be overdone, especially on a wide door as the parts may be forced out of flat.

Fine strong canvas is glued over the whole. Assuming Scotch glue to be used it may be that it will chill before the job can be completed. In this case it can be warmed afresh by holding an electric radiator over it, or by passing a warm iron over the canvas with a damp cloth interposed. If the joints are close there is no danger of glue penetrating them and sticking the parts together. If there is any doubt about it the edges of the strips should be rubbed over with a piece of candle grease. When the glue has hardened the joints can

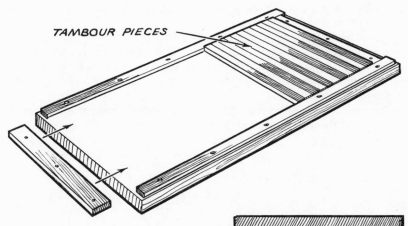

TAMBOUR PIECES

Fig. 24 (*above*). ASSEMBLING
TAMBOUR STRIPS

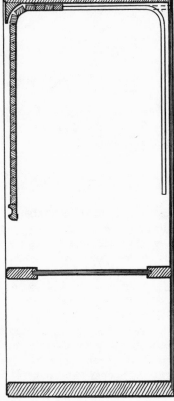

Fig. 25. SECTION THROUGH
CARCASE SHOWING TAMBOUR
WHICH RISES VERTICALLY

be broken by passing the whole canvas side downwards over any rounded object such as a thick dowel.

Sometimes the tambour has to be fitted around a bow-front job, and the normal sight position is around the curve. If the tambour were assembled on a flat board the joints would be slightly open when on the curve. Consequently a cradle for assembling should be made, the curve being the same as in the job itself.

In some cases the end of the tambour consists of a stouter member, possibly to take a lock. It may be more convenient to add this afterwards,

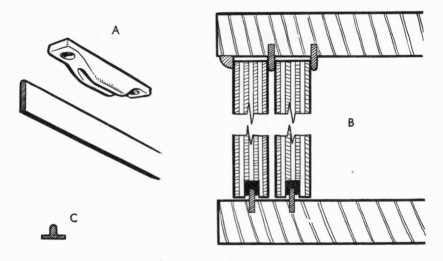

Fig. 26. SLIDING DOORS WITH GLIDERS

but generally there is a rebate and the canvas can be glued to it straightway. Most tambour doors curve in one direction only, and the rectangular section is quite successful To be able to feed in the tambour it is usually necessary to cut an exit groove at the back, as shown by the dotted lines in Fig. 25, this being filled in after the tambour has been fed in. It will be realized that square-edged sections will bend in one direction only.

Sliding Doors

These are little different from hinged doors in construction but allowance has to be made for the method of sliding. Today the usual method is to use one of the proprietary tracks and gliders as shown at (A), Fig. 26. This enables the door to move easily and silently. A groove is cut along the bottom edge of the door, not to engage the track but to give clearance for it (B). The gliders are screwed in this groove, the depth being so arranged that the bottom of the door clears the cupboard bottom by about $\frac{1}{16}$ in. The two doors must clear each other by about $\frac{1}{16}$ in. also, assuming that good, reliable material is used. If it is inclined to twist rather more should be allowed.

The track itself may either fit into grooves (B, Fig. 26) or be screwed direct to the bottom (C), in which case an edging is usually added at front to conceal the gap and keep out dirt. At the top no track is needed, but it is necessary to fit separating beads to keep the top of the door in position (B). The beads can be inserted after the doors are in position. The door itself can be any of the usual forms, flush or framed.

In another way the track can be made from a close-grained hardwood which will resist wear. In this case hardwood blocks (which are virtually gliders) are screwed in at each end. A deep groove is cut in the door and the hardwood block screwed to this, the screws being deeply countersunk. In this way only the hardwood blocks engage the track which is flat at the top. The idea is shown in Fig. 27.

Another form of proprietary mechanism is a metal fitting with ball-bearings running on a metal track. It is more suitable for heavy doors but is noisier in action.

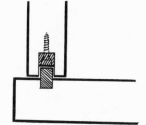

Fig. 27. HARDWOOD BLOCK USED AS A
A GLIDER FOR SLIDING DOOR

7 Veneering

THERE IS MORE veneering being done at the present time than at any other period, largely because it is impossible to obtain many woods except in veneer form, and also because materials suitable for grounds can be obtained in large sizes, whereas originally solid wood had to be used. Properly done, veneering is a perfectly reliable and legitimate process—in fact it is the only means whereby certain decorative and attractive effects can be obtained. For instance, cross-banded and built-up designs such as quartering could not be carried out in any other way. The fact that it has been used as a cheap way of

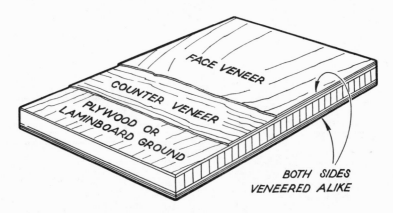

Fig. 1. BLOCKBOARD GROUNDWORK WITH COUNTER VENEER AT RIGHT ANGLES WITH GROUND AND FACE VENEER

covering up poor materials and workmanship does not invalidate its proper use. There are, however, certain pitfalls, for it should be remembered that the test of veneering is not what the job looks like immediately when finished, but what it is like a few years later. It is inevitable that any faults in either materials or construction will show themselves eventually.

118

Groundwork

Good quality plywood and lamin board make good grounds because they are obtainable in wide panels and are free from shrinkage. Common tea-chest ply, however, is useless. There may be either obvious or hidden faults, and, although the latter may not immediately show as blemishes, they will eventually reveal themselves. Thus the inner layers may have open joints which eventually cause sinking, or they may be overlapped, resulting in the parts being under pressure, causing a high ridge eventually to appear. Gaboon ply is usually reliable as a groundwork.

Whenever practicable the grain of the veneer should be at right angles with that of the outer layers of the plywood. The reason is that in manufacture the layers of the ply are peeled from the log rotary fashion, and are necessarily opened out flat when made up as plywood. This often results in hair cracks being formed at the surface which tend to open with drying. If the veneer is in the same direction as the outer layers the moisture in the glue causes swelling and consequent closing of the cracks. Then, as the moisture dries out,

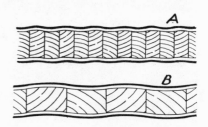

Fig. 2. WAVINESS SHOWN IN EXAGGERATION OF (A) LAMIN BOARD AND (B) BLOCKBOARD

they open afresh and drag the newly laid veneer with it, causing fine cracks to open.

For good class work the surfaces are counter-veneered; that is, a sheet of veneer is laid at right angles with the groundwork, and the final veneer at right angles with this. Fig. 1 shows the idea.

There are occasions when the rule has to be broken. For instance in built-up patterns such as quartering the grain direction necessarily varies, and the only positive way is to counter-veneer across the grain first.

Exactly the same applies when lamin board is used, the grain direction of the veneer being at right angles with that of the outer layers. There are three main types of this board; batten board, blockboard, and lamin board, the difference being in the width of the core strips. Of the three the best for veneering is lamin board in which the strips have a maximum width of 7 mm. It will be realized that, owing to shrinkage, waves are liable to appear on the surface as shown in Fig. 2, and the narrower the layers the smaller these will be. They can, in fact, be easily sanded out in lamin board. In any case the board should be kept in stock for as long as possible before use, and be toothed or coarse sanded immediately before veneering. Blockboard has a maximum core strip width of 1 in., and batten board 3 in.

Solid wood can be used providing it is reliable and free from blemishes. In the case of softwood it is generally advisable to size it first as otherwise it soaks up the glue, leaving the veneer starved. Any knots must be chopped out

Fig. 3. USING TOOTHING PLANE ON GROUNDWORK

and replaced by little fillings of sound wood. Clean pine which is flat and brought to a moisture content of about 12 per cent is quite successful. Of the hardwoods, straight-grained mahogany, agba, mansonia, obeche, and beech all make good grounds. Oak is often used but its rather coarse grain is liable to show through to the surface of thin veneer eventually.

Preparation of Groundwork

It is obviously important that the groundwork is made perfectly flat, and solid wood should be planed perfectly true and finally gone over in all directions with the toothing plane (Fig. 3). This not only gives a key to the glue, but takes out any inequalities left by the plane. A safe rule in all veneering is to treat both sides of the groundwork alike. A less expensive veneer can be used at the back, but it should be of the same thickness and laid in the same direction. Sometimes it is possible to veneer on one side only, especially when the wood is held rigidly by other parts of the structure, as, for instance, in the ends of a carcase which are held by the top and bottom, etc., but free items such as doors, table-tops, and so on should certainly be veneered both sides.

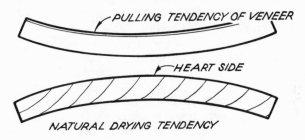

Fig. 4. PULLING TENDENCY OF VENEER OPPOSED TO DRYING TENDENCY (SHOWN IN EXAGGERATION)

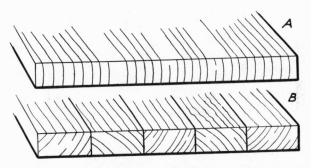

Fig. 5. TWO TYPES OF SOLID GROUNDWORK

Good quality chipboard makes a successful groundwork. Its disadvantage for handwork is that is is awkward to trim to size, and should whenever possible be cut dead to size on the circular saw. Here again for first class work counter-veneering is advisable.

Minimizing Pull of Veneer

It is true that certain precautions can be taken to minimize the ever-present tendency of veneer to pull the groundwork hollow. The reason for this latter tendency is that the moisture in the glue causes the veneer to swell, and as it dries out to shrink again. As by this time it has gripped the wood it pulls the latter hollow. The only completely reliable way is to veneer both sides so that the pull is equalized. In the case of solid wood it is a help to lay the veneer

121

on the heart side because the natural tendency of wood is to shrink away from the heart side as Fig. 4 shows.

Assuming that both sides of solid wood are being veneered it is a help to use quarter-cut wood because this has no natural tendency to twist one way or the other (A), Fig. 5. If this is not practicable it is better to use narrow stuff and joint it together with the heart sides alternated as at (B). The result of any twisting may be that the surface may undulate slightly, but there should not be any serious pulling hollow.

Originally there were two kinds of veneer; saw-cut and knife-cut. The former was thicker, nearly $\frac{1}{16}$ in., but today is entirely unobtainable, largely owing to the tremendous wastage in sawdust. Nearly all decorative hardwoods are flat-sliced or half rotary sliced. Plain veneers such as are used in plywood making, however, are rotary sliced, the log being mounted in a lathe-like machine and the veneer unwrapped as it were. Such veneers have a wild and uninteresting grain as the cut is more or less parallel with the annual rings.

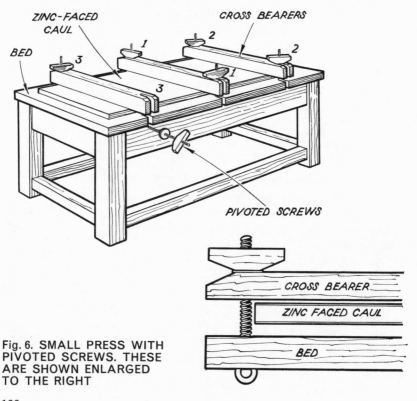

Fig. 6. SMALL PRESS WITH PIVOTED SCREWS. THESE ARE SHOWN ENLARGED TO THE RIGHT

Methods of Veneering
There are three main methods of veneering; machine press, caul, and hammer veneering. The first two have much in common, but, since machine presses are expensive, their use is confined to trade workshops.

Machine Presses
These include heavily built appliances hand-operated by large screws, multi-platen presses hydraulically operated, and rubber bag installations by means of which shaped work can be pressed without any special formers. An example of a small press is that in Fig. 6 which consists of a main bed on an under-frame. Around the edges are stout screws with large wing-nuts operating over slotted cross-bearers with slightly bowed lower edges. These bearers press down over a zinc-faced caul. The work may be placed either veneer side upper-most or downwards. When both sides are to be veneered both veneers are put

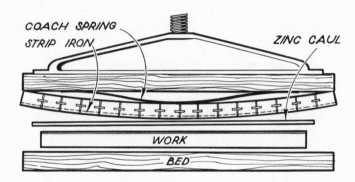

Fig. 7. ARRANGEMENT OF LARGE SCREW PRESS

down in one operation, and a pair of cauls is used. The order of tightening the screws is important because the purpose is to drive surplus glue out at the edges. Note the order in Fig. 6 in which the middle ones are tightened first.

When large panels are being veneered in a big press it may happen that glue is trapped in the middle of the panel, and it is often a help to follow the idea in Fig. 7 in which a series of wood cross-members of equal thickness is attached to curved leaf springs. Thus when the screw is tightened the pressure is felt in the middle first, and the glue driven outwards. A zinc caul is placed over the veneer beneath the boards.

Cauls
It will be realized that individual panels can be veneered one or both sides in

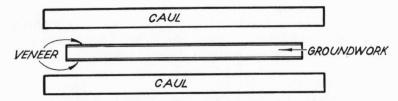

Fig. 8. VENEERING BOTH SIDES SIMULTANEOUSLY

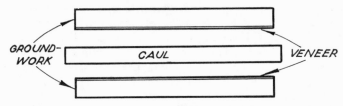

Fig. 9. ONE SIDE OF TWO PANELS VENEERED AT SAME TIME

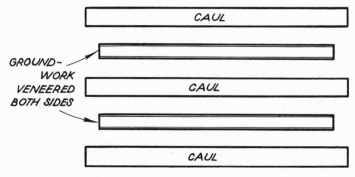

Fig. 10. BOTH SIDES OF TWO PANELS VENEERED TOGETHER

one operation. Two cauls are needed for both sides as in Fig. 8. Furthermore, two panels can be veneered one side by the use of a single caul (Fig. 9), or two panels can be veneered both sides by the use of three cauls (Fig. 10). The cauls themselves can be either of wood or zinc backed with wood. Assuming Scotch glue to be used the cauls need to be thoroughly heated beforehand, and it is therefore obviously useless to use plywood or blockboard which has been assembled with animal glue for the cauls. Marine quality ply would be successful because it is put together with resin glue. If solid wood is used any joints in it to increase the width should be strengthened in some way. Single face cauls could have cross-battens at the back to stiffen them. On the whole it is more satisfactory to use zinc-faced cauls as they retain the heat better, and present a perfectly flat surface.

The screw press is also manufactured in large size and in multiple form. Many panels can be dealt with in one operation, but it is still advisable to use the leaf spring idea to avoid trapping glue in the middle. The press can also be used for special work requiring the use of jigs as in some shaped work. Some older presses had a steel plate at the bottom which could be gas heated.

Whilst on the subject of presses, mention may be made of the large multi-platten type used for pressing many panels in one operation. They are usually thermostatically controlled, so that the heat can be regulated. The chief benefit in this comes when resin glue is used which is cured by heat. Thus the panels can be inserted cold, pressure applied, and the heat turned on. In a minute or so the glue has set, thus freeing the press for a further set of panels. Such a press is used only in large workshops.

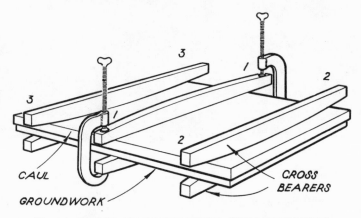

Fig. 11. ORDER OF TIGHTENING CROSS-BEARERS
The centre bearers have been tightened and their inner edges are thus bent flat

Another type of machine press found in the latter is the rubber bag type used for shaped work. There is a main bed on which the work is placed, and a rubber sheet which is drawn over the whole. Paper is interposed to prevent adhesion. A domed cover is placed over the whole and held with heavy bolts having wing nuts. Air is forced in at the top causing the rubber to take up to the shape of the work and press evenly over the whole. The use of a reverse former is thus avoided. Another type of press draws the air from beneath the sheet so that the rubber sheet is forced down by atmospheric pressure.

125

Caul Veneering

Unless a lot of veneering is normally done the installations of even a simple press is not worth while. This means that the work has to be done by either the caul or the hammer method. The caul is simply a flat piece of wood, $\frac{1}{2}$ in. to 1 in. thick according to the size, and slightly larger than the panel being veneered. As it has to be made really hot (assuming Scotch glue to be used)

Fig. 12. USE OF THE VENEERING HAMMER

it is essential to strengthen any joints in it as otherwise they may fail when heated.

The procedure is to glue both groundwork and veneer, lay the latter in position, and put several sheets of newspaper on top. The caul is now thoroughly heated on both sides. Unless this is done the heat is soon lost and may fail to liquefy the glue. Without loss of time the caul is placed over the newspaper and cramped down by means of several pairs of cross-bearers. These last-named are slightly curved along their inner edges as shown in exaggeration in Fig. 11. In this way the pressure is felt in the centre first so that the glue is squeezed outwards. For the same reason the centre cross-bearers are always tightened first.

When both sides of a panel have to be veneered they should be dealt with simultaneously in one operation, two cauls being used as in Fig. 8. If a pair of panels are veneered one side only they can be dealt with at the same time, a single caul being used as in Fig. 9. Pairs of panels to be dealt with together need three cauls as in Fig. 10. For such operations the help of an assistant is invariably necessary, otherwise the heat may be lost before the cramps can be tightened. Provision for heating the three cauls simultaneously is also essential.

In all this work the cramps should remain tightened for about an hour after which they can be slackened.

Hammer Veneering

The groundwork is prepared as already explained and glue applied to both it and the veneer. The latter is placed in position and about half of the upper surface lightly damped with a moist swab. A flat iron is made just warm enough to liquefy the glue, is passed over the surface and the veneering hammer (Fig. 12) worked with a zig-zag movement from the centre outwards, the object being to squeeze out surplus glue at the edges and to bring the veneer into close contact with the groundwork.

Avoiding Casting

The tendency of veneer to pull work hollow has already been mentioned. This is owing to the swelling of the veneer and the subsequent drying out. It follows, then, that any precautions taken to prevent this double movement in the veneer is bound to be helpful. This includes the use of the minimum amount of moisture, the avoidance of undue stretching by the action of the veneering hammer, and having the iron hot enough to only just liquefy the glue. Too hot an iron causes the moisture to be converted into steam, which in turn makes the veneer extra pliable and so liable to stretch. Different woods vary in the treatment required, however, some needing more moisture than others.

Flatting Veneers

Veneers should be stored with a flat board pressed down by a heavy weight on top. Otherwise they are liable to buckle. If a badly buckled leaf has to be laid, especially by caul or press, it is necessary to flat it first as otherwise it will crack under pressure. In most cases it is enough to damp both sides to make the veneer pliable, and cramp between two heated flat boards. After an hour or two the veneer will have dried out flat. Sometimes the process may have to be repeated.

This treatment is sometimes too drastic, especially when the buckling is bad, and it is then better to damp both sides with thin glue size, place between two flat boards (cold) and put a heavy weight on top. If left overnight the veneers are generally flat, though here again the process may have to be repeated.

Jointing

In caul or press veneering all jointing to make up width or to form decorative patterns is done beforehand. The parts are fitted neatly together and held with a strip of gummed tape. It is then laid as a single sheet. This is impracticable in hammer veneering, and the joining veneers are laid with an overlap of about ½ in., as at (A), Fig. 13. A straight-edge is cramped down over the overlap, and a cut made through both thicknesses with a thin, keen chisel, a knife, (B). This enables the waste of the upper piece to be peeled away straightway, and, by raising the other side, the waste of the lower veneer

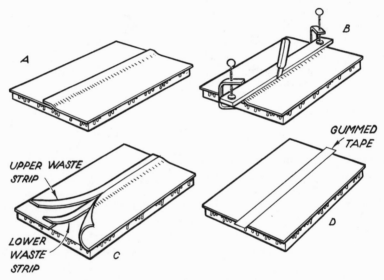

Fig. 13. MAKING A JOINT WHEN HAMMER VENEERING

can be reached and pulled away (C). When the veneer is pressed down a perfect joint is formed. It is advisable to pass the iron down the joint to warm up the glue afresh, and a strip of gummed tape should be stuck over the joint to prevent it from opening as the moisture dries out (D).

When a panel has to be cross-banded the centre veneer is laid first. It should stand in all round, but should be large enough to extend into the cross-banding. A cutting gauge is sharpened to a keen edge, and set to the width of the cross-banding. A cut with this all round enables the waste to be peeled away (A), Fig. 14. Strips of veneer cut across the grain are then fitted up, being mitred at the corners and butted together (B). Again gummed tape is stuck over all joints.

Counter-veneering

It should be realized that both sides of the panel must be treated alike if the work is to remain flat. In the case of caul or press veneering it is possible to lay both counter- and face-veneer on both sides simultaneously when the panel is small and the veneers flat without joints. Generally, however, it is necessary to lay the counter-veneers first and the face-veneers afterwards. This enables the tapes necessary in any joints to be removed and the surfaces to be toothed lightly before the face-veneers are laid. Furthermore, if any blemishes such as a pimple caused by any extraneous matter beneath are present these can be put right.

In the case of hammer-veneering, the groundwork having been prepared on both sides, the two counter-veneers are laid, one immediately after the other, the grain at right angles with the groundwork. The glue is allowed to dry out when the two surfaces are lightly toothed. It is then regarded as though it were a simple solid panel and the two face-veneers laid. Providing the iron is not made too hot there is no danger of the counter-veneer lifting.

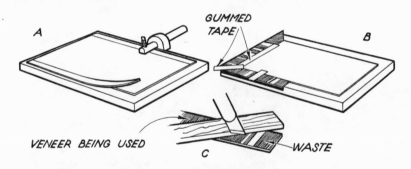

Fig. 14. LAYING A CROSS-BANDING

Glues for Veneering

In the trade resin glue is often used, being extended with rye flour to cheapen the cost. Either the press or caul must be used, and in the former case there is an advantage in that the glue can be cured quickly by heat in the platens, enabling the press to be freed quickly for further panels. Since, however, it is impossible to re-liquefy the glue it is obvious that the procedure must be positive because any blemishes that may occur cannot be put right. For this reason Scotch glue is advisable for the man who has no professional facilities or experience. A second advantage of Scotch glue is that it can be used equally well for press, caul, or hammer-veneering—in fact, it is the only glue for which the hammer method can be used.

Fig. 15. CUTTING VENEER WITH CHISEL OR KNIFE

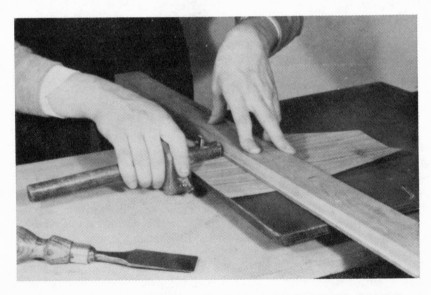

Fig. 16. CUTTING PARALLEL STRIPS WITH CUTTING GAUGE

Fig. 17. TRIMMING VENEER ON SHOOTING BOARD

Sometimes casein glue is used in the press or caul, but it has the drawback of being liable to stain many hardwoods, which means that all traces of glue must be kept from the face of the veneer. Furthermore, open-grained or thin veneers are liable to penetration by the glue, this again causing face staining. If it is used it is advisable to place several thicknesses of newspaper between the veneer and the caul to soak up any possible penetration. Even the glue labelled 'non-staining' is liable to the trouble. It is true that the stains can often be bleached out later with oxalic acid (poisonous) but it is better to avoid the trouble, as the final result may still tend to be patchy.

Cutting and Trimming

Veneer should be placed on a flat board and cut with a keen knife or chisel worked against a straight-edge as in Fig. 15. When several strips are needed as in cross-banding it can be cut with the cutting gauge from each side, Fig. 16. Note the batten to prevent buckling. To trim the edge the shooting board is used, Fig. 17, the batten again being used.

After laying the surface is cleaned up with the scraper followed by glasspaper. The latter is used in the direction of the grain except for such woods as burr walnut when only the finest grade glasspaper is used with a circular movement. In built-up patterns the glasspaper is used in one direction only and only a fine grade used. The orbital sander is excellent for this work.

131

8 Screws, Nails, Bolts, Adhesives

THERE IS A wide range of fixings designed for various purposes, the choice depending upon the requirements of the job itself.

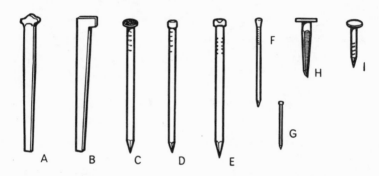

Fig. 1. RANGE OF NAILS USED IN WOODWORK
A. Cut-clasp. B. Cut. C. French wire. D. Lost head. E. Oval brad. F. Panel pin.
G. Veneer pin. H. Tack. I. Wire clout

Nails

These are made in a huge variety of forms and sizes. In some jobs strength is the only consideration—carpentry, for instance. In others appearance may be equally important, and a fine nail that shows very little when driven in is needed. Some of the commonest are shown in Fig. 1. When strength is essential the cut clasp-nail at (A) is the best. The cut-nail (B) is also strong but is neater and also has the advantage of not being so liable to split the wood when driven in near the edge.

French wire nails (C) have a strong grip but leave a somewhat unsightly hole, and are used on carpentry jobs where appearance is of secondary importance. They can be made less unsightly by laying the head on a metal block and hammering flat (Fig. 2). However, it is better in this case to use lost head-nails (D), although they are more liable to pull through.

A nail with reasonable strength, yet still neat, is the oval brad (E). The head should be in line with the grain. For lighter work the panel pin (F) is widely used. When punched in it shows little. The veneer pin (G) is for still lighter work—in fact, its purpose is usually to hold parts temporarily whilst the glue sets.

Tacks (H) are needed mostly in upholstery and similar work. The improved type has a larger head than the standard and is better. For roofing felt the wire clout nail (I) is widely used. For outdoor work it should be galvanized.

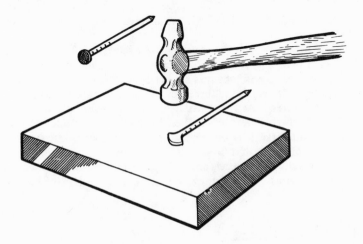

Fig. 2. FLATTENING HEAD OF FRENCH NAIL

The force of blow used when nailing is a matter of judgment, and is something that comes only with practice. Keep the hammer face clean, as grease or dirt is the commonest cause of nails bending. An occasional rub on glasspaper is all that is wanted. On anything but rough carpentry cease striking when the nail is a trifle proud of the surface and finish off with the punch. Otherwise the wood surface is liable to be bruised. In some rough carpentry jobs where strength is essential the nails are often taken right through and clenched at the back, especially in softwood.

Screws

Apart from the metal of which they are made, there are three main types of screws as shown in Fig. 3, countersunk, round-head, and raised-head. The diagram also shows where the size is taken from. Gauge is the diameter of the

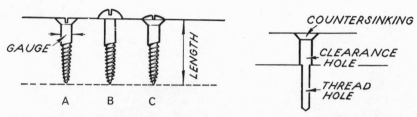

Fig. 3. TYPE OF SCREWS AND
WHERE SIZE IS TAKEN FROM

Fig. 4. HOLES NEEDED
WHEN SCREWING

shank beneath the head. All details should be given when ordering screws as follows:

'Three dozen $1\frac{3}{4}$ in. countersunk, iron, twelves.'

Two sizes of holes are needed when screwing; the clearance hole through which the shank passes and which is a trifle larger than the shank diameter; and the thread hole in which the thread bites, this the same size as the core at the centre of the thread. As the resistance when screwing into hard wood is considerable it is highly desirable, when brass screws have to be used, to drive in an iron one first. It is then withdrawn and the brass one substituted. In any case the thread should be greased so that friction is reduced as far as possible. Incidentally, iron screws are liable to rust in oak owing to a chemical reaction. If they must be used they should be given a coat of vaseline or tallow first.

Fig. 5. CARRIAGE BOLT

For some heavy work where their appearance is not a disadvantage carriage bolts are useful. They have domed heads with a square part immediately beneath, and when used in softwood the latter bites into the wood without special cutting. The square prevents the bolt from turning when the nut is tightened. It is imperative that a washer is used beneath the latter. For such work as holding together the sides of sheds, coal bunkers, etc., they are excellent.

Although intended primarily for handrails, the handrail bolt has other uses, notably for fixing mitres in heavy timbers such as in kerbs, etc. Holes are bored in the joining faces to take the bolt itself, and slots are recessed at the back of the wood to hold the nuts, one of which is square. The latter is dropped in, the bolt turned into it, and the round nut placed in the other slot. The projecting end of the bolt is entered into its hole, and the round nut turned by a special punch or even with a screwdriver passed into the grooves around the edge. A dowel is also advisable to prevent any twisting tendency, Fig. 6.

ADHESIVES

Animal Glue

This is generally known as Scotch glue, although there are proprietary glues which are of animal origin. It is obtainable in cake, pearl, or powder form, but all become alike when melted down and thinned with water. The cake type has to be broken up and takes longer to prepare, hence the increasing popularity of the second two types.

It is a strong glue, free from staining, but not water-resistant. Consequently it cannot be used for outdoor work. It needs to be used hot, and this

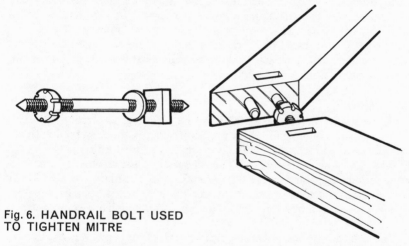

Fig. 6. HANDRAIL BOLT USED
TO TIGHTEN MITRE

involves warming the parts to be joined to avoid chilling, and if possible assembling in a warm workshop. Furthermore the work needs to be gone about speedily so that everything is in the final position whilst the glue is still liquid. Except for small jobs this generally involves having assistance, partly to warm the parts, and also to hold and adjust cramps. It is an excellent veneering glue, and, in fact, for the hammer method, the only one that can be used.

To prepare it the glue is placed in the container, covered with water, and left overnight. It is heated with hot water (never a naked flame). Cleanliness is important, rust and dirt being avoided because, apart from making the glue dirty, it may cause staining. This, incidentally, should be remembered in the hot-water container. Dirty, rust-laden water may easily cause oak and other hardwoods to become badly stained. An excellent way is to put the glue in a jam jar or earthenware jar, and heat this in a saucepan of water. The glass will not crack if the glue level is always above that of the water.

Animal glue should never be boiled. Its optimum temperature is in the region of 140 degrees F. which is about 20 degrees hotter than the hottest water one can wash comfortably in. Some proprietary glues do not need much heating.

Casein Glue

Cold application gives this an advantage over animal glue, but as it has no natural tackiness it is not practicable to make rubbed joints; they have to be cramped. Furthermore it is liable to stain certain hardwoods—even the so-called non-staining varieties—and a dark glue line may result, as well as marks due to squeezed-out glue. Such marks can usually be taken out with oxalic acid (poisonous), but it is better to avoid staining as the surrounding timber may also be lightened. It is more damp-resistant than animal glue but is not waterproof. For purposes in which the glue joints are concealed, for painted work, or woods which are not liable to be stained, it is a strong glue, giving ample assembly time.

Resin Glue

There are several advantages in this adhesive; it has great strength, is highly water-resistant, is non-staining, is used cold (that is the urea type normally available in small quantities), and gives ample assembly time.

It is put up in various forms. The type used in the trade is a fairly thick syrup with separate hardener. No setting takes place until the two are brought into contact. Its disadvantage for the small user is that it has a limited shelf life, somewhere in the region of three months, after which it becomes rubbery and unusable.

The same adhesive is also available in powder form, however, and this has a very much longer shelf life. It is mixed with water when it becomes the syrup already referred to. This glue is generally used with the separate application method, the glue being applied to the one part of the joint, and the hardener to the other. There is thus considerable assembly time because setting does not start until the two are brought together.

Another type of glue in powder form has the hardener already incorporated. This again has a long shelf life and requires only to be mixed with water. Only enough glue for immediate purposes should be mixed up because it becomes unusable once setting is seriously under way. There is, however, ample time for most assembly jobs.

The latest form of resin glue is a white syrup in which does not require a hardener. It sets quickly and has great strength but is not water resistant.

All of these glues should be kept free from metal as contamination can cause staining. Thus it should be mixed in a glass, earthenware, or plastic container, and a brush without a metal ferrule used. Iron cramps should not touch the surface of the wood where glue has squeezed out. Veneering with caul or press is practicable but not the hammer method, as it cannot be re-liquefied.

Polyvinyl Acetate

Here is another cold-application glue ready for use as it is. It is strong and fairly resistant to damp, but may suffer from creep; that is a heavy panel glued in a vertical position may gradually drop by its own weight over a long period. It is white in colour, but some makes are liable to darken when in contact with certain woods. Thus, although they may not cause actual staining of the wood, the glue itself may show as a dark line. With dark woods this does not matter. It is not ideal for veneering because the thin spread would set before the two could be brought into contact.

Rubber-based Adhesives

So far as woodwork is concerned the chief use of these is in bonding plastic sheets to wood. It is impossible to use it for framing joints because it grabs on contact and the parts could not be slid into position. For a plastic sheet, it is important that it is positioned exactly, and that no air is trapped beneath. As a rule the simplest way is to fix projecting strips around two edges at right angles and hold the plastic sheet against these as it is lowered. It is a help to bend the sheet so that no air is trapped.

Another use is in some repair work in which it would be difficult to fix cramps—elaborate carving, for instance. The immediate grab prevents any tendency to drop away. It is usually known as contact adhesive.

9 Fittings

FOR FURNITURE-MAKING these are invariably of brass, sometimes chromium-plated but frequently left plain. The quality in many instances has sadly deteriorated—in fact, it is often impossible to obtain really good fittings. For house doors, etc., iron fittings are invariably used.

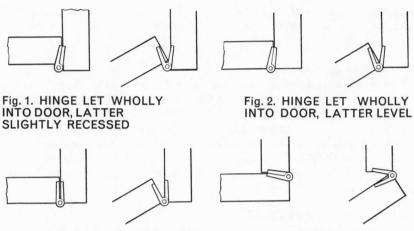

Fig. 1. HINGE LET WHOLLY
INTO DOOR, LATTER
SLIGHTLY RECESSED

Fig. 2. HINGE LET WHOLLY
INTO DOOR, LATTER LEVEL

Fig. 3. HINGE LET EQUALLY
INTO DOOR AND CARCASE

Fig. 4. DOOR CLOSING OVER
FRONT OF CARCASE

HINGES

Butt Hinges

The solid drawn type should always be used. Cheaper bent hinges are useless as they soon fail. For most purposes the butt hinge is used, and is normally available in sizes from 1 in. up to 3 in. in brass, and $1\frac{1}{2}$ in. to 5 in. in iron. For cabinet doors it can be fitted in two ways; wholly into the door, or equally into door and cupboard according to circumstances. Sometimes either way is satisfactory.

Fig. 1 shows the hinge let entirely into the door and is clearly the only practicable method since the door is set back from the face slightly. Note that the centre of the pin projects from the door face at least half the amount of the set-in of the door, thus enabling the door to open through 180 degrees. If the door were flush with the cabinet face the centre of the pin could align with the front of the door, as in Fig. 2, or alternatively the hinge could be let equally into both door and cabinet as in Fig. 3, again with the pin centre level with the face. When the door closes over the face of the cabinet it is usual to let the hinge entirely into the door as in Fig. 4, and to work a small bead along the door edge in line with the hinge.

A point to note in all the cases where the hinge is let in its entirety into the door is that the edge of the flange is also recessed at an angle into the cabinet. This does not affect the movement of the hinge as the centre is unaffected, but it has the advantage of being stronger since the recess gives definite support, whereas without the recess it relies entirely upon the screws. Furthermore, it is neater since the flange edge is let in flush.

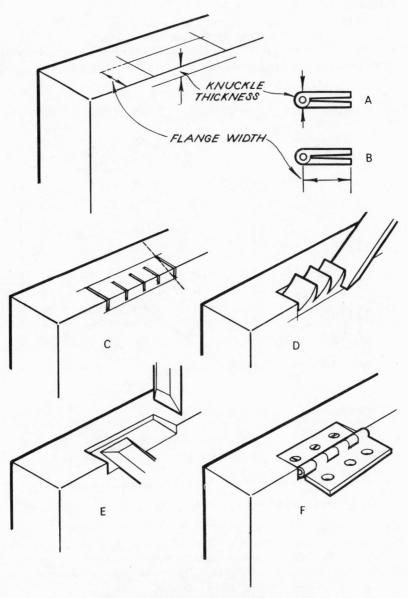

Fig. 5. STAGES IN RECESSING HINGES

Fitting Butt Hinges

First decide on the hinge position. There is no definite rule, but a general guide is to fix them their own length from the top and bottom. Square one line across the edge of the wood in pencil, place the hinge up to the line and mark the other end again squaring the line across the edge. Assuming that the

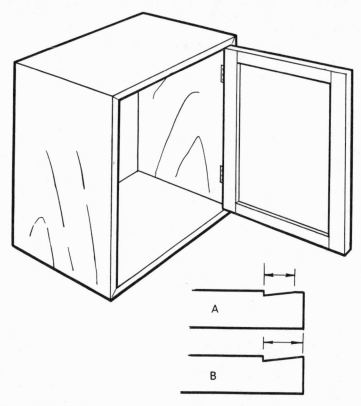

Fig. 6. TRANSFERRING MARKS FROM DOOR TO CARCASE

hinge is to be let in its entirety into the door, the gauge is set to the exact thickness of the hinge at the knuckle and the door marked as in Fig. 5(A). If the door is to be flush with the cabinet front (Fig. 3) a second gauge is set to the flange width from the edge to the centre of the pin (B), Fig. 5. If it is to stand in, the gauge is set short of this distance by half the amount of the set-in and the door marked.

A saw cut is made at each end as far down as the diagonal, and several intermediate cuts to break up the grain (C). The ends are chopped down, and a further cut made along the gauge line. A series of cuts is made with the chisel and mallet, again to break up the grain (D), after which the waste can be pared away as at (E). The hinge is now fixed with a couple of screws (F).

To transfer the marks to the cabinet the door is held in position, as in Fig. 6, and marks made at each end of the hinges. These marks are squared in in pencil and the gauge reset to give the required set-in of the door (A). If it is to be flush it has the same setting (B). Sloping notches have to be cut to receive the flanges, only the edge of the flange fitting flush. A single screw only is driven into each hinge and the door tested before the final screws are put in.

When the hinge is being let equally into both door and cabinet the gauge

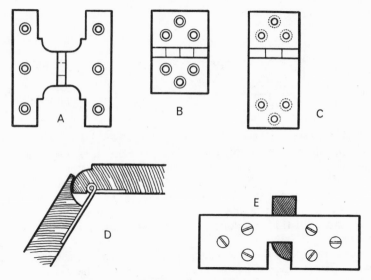

Fig. 7. TYPES OF HINGES
A. Parliament hinges. B. Back flaps. C. Table-top hinges. D. Rule joint of drop-leaf table. E. Scratch stock and cutter for rule joint

is set to the centre of the pin and both parts marked with the same setting. A point to note when hingeing is that binding (that is, the door springing open after closing) is usually caused by the hinge recesses being cut in too deeply, or by too large a gauge of screw being used so that the heads foul each other.

A problem that sometimes arises is in the case of shaped work. A parallel example is that of railway carriage doors. Ordinary hingeing is not practicable because the parts would foul each other. It is necessary to set out the parts in full size, at any rate in plan and plot the closed and open positions so that the movement is unrestricted. It invariably means that the hinge centres have to project from the face of the work to give this clearance. All hingeing centres have to be vertically in line, and if the curve of the job varies in different parts (as in a railway carriage) all hinges may need a different projection from the face of the work.

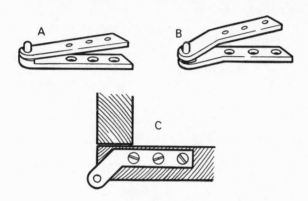

Fig. 8. CENTRE
HINGES
A. Straight
B. Cranked
C. Cranked type,
    in position

Much the same problem arises when there are projecting members on the face of the job. For instance, in the folding room door with a large architrave and skirting it is necessary to use parliament hinges which project well from the face of the door (A), Fig. 7. For these it is necessary to put the centre of the knuckle at slightly more than half the distance of the greatest projection. Thus if the latter (say, the architrave) is $1\frac{1}{2}$ in. thick, the knuckle centre would project, say, $\frac{7}{8}$ in. If in any doubt, the simplest way is to set out the work in full size.

Similar in type to the butt hinge, but much wider, is the back flap hinge shown at (B). It is used for items such as bureau falls where the width is not so restricted.

A variation of this is the table fall hinge (C)—used for the drop-leaf table, the edge having the rule joint (D). The advantage of the latter is that in the up position the leaf is supported throughout its length by the form of the moulded edge, not merely by the screws of the hinges. A second point is its neatness. As it involves the knuckle being recessed into the wood the countersinking for the screws has to be on the reverse side.

A section through the edge should be set out, the centre of the pin being the centre from which the curve of the moulded edge is set out. The width of the square section can be anything within reason. If too wide it looks clumsy, whereas a narrow one is damaged easily. For an oak top about $\frac{7}{8}$ in. thick it

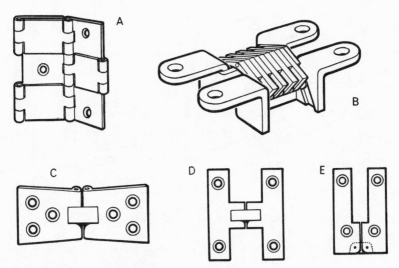

Fig. 9. TYPES OF HINGES
A. Screen. B. Soss. C. Counter. D, E. Card table

can be about $\frac{1}{8}$ in. and rather less for mahogany. It is possible to obtain a pair of planes for working the moulded edge, but the rebate plane can be used for the round member, and a round plane for the hollow. A pair of scratch cutters is made which coincide with shape exactly, and these used in the scratch-stock to finish off. It is an advantage to make the special stock with two shoulders as at (E), Fig. 7, as it prevents drifting away from the edge.

Centre Hinges
These can often be used in place of butt hinges, but more frequently when a special centre is needed. One point to remember is that it is generally neces-sary to be able to move either the top above or the bottom beneath in order to be able to fit the hinge, though there are occasions when it is possible to place the hinge in position on the carcase and slide the door in. One essential feature is that when a loose top is fitted (a cornice, for instance) it must be screwed down. Otherwise an accidental lift would enable the door to fall forwards.

There are two kinds of centre hinges (Fig. 8), straight (A) and cranked (B). The last-named are used when the pivoting centre has to align with the outer corner of the door as at (C). This enables the door to swing clear of any other moving part such as another door. Both kinds are made in pairs, top and bottom. The latter has either a raised shoulder or is fitted with a washer so that the two parts of the hinge clear each other.

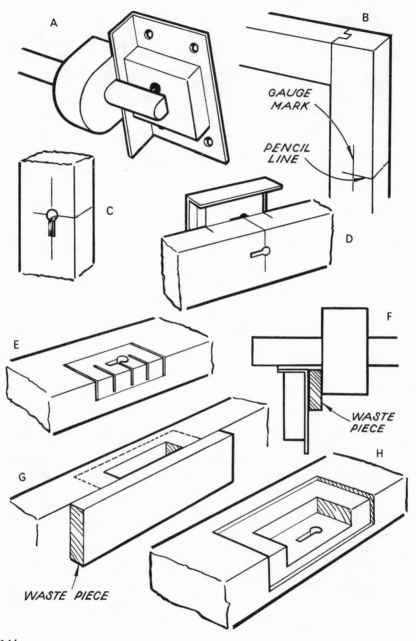

GAUGE MARK

PENCIL LINE

WASTE PIECE

WASTE PIECE

Various Hinges

Screen hinges enable the leaves of a screen to fold either way. It is essential that the thickness of the wood equals or is a trifle less than the distance between the pin centres. If too thin there will be a gap between the folds when the screen is open. If too thick, the screen will bind as it is opened. The hinge is shown at (A), Fig. 9.

Ordinary decorative hinges such as the butterfly call for no special remark as they are merely screwed on the surface.

A hinge which has become popular of late is the soss (B) which is used mainly for table leaves. Its special feature is that there are no projecting knuckles. It is, however, considerably more expensive and unless its features have a special advantage for the job in hand there is little point in using it.

For counters and some tables which have a leaf which folds upwards it is necessary to have a double-throw hinge which again has no projecting knuckle at the top, so that there is nothing standing up at the top to prevent items from lying flat. It is shown at (C). Its dovetail shape adds considerably to the strength in that it resists drag.

Another form of double-throw hinge is the card table hinge, which may be centre pattern (D), or the end (E). In both cases the top is free of all projections. Both are let flush into the wood.

LOCKS

These are of various kinds to suit the particular purpose for which they are needed. The simplest kind is screwed straight on at the inside of the door, and usually can be fitted to either a right- or left-hand door since the bolt shoots either way. Most cabinet locks are the cut type, however, and need to be let flush into the wood. These are right- and left-hand. To tell which is needed: face the closed door, and if the lock is on the left-hand stile a left-hand lock is needed, and vice versa.

Fitting the Cut Lock

To fit a lock of this kind, square a pencil line across the face and edge of the door stile. Set a gauge to the distance in of the lock-pin from the plate (A), Fig. 10, and cut the pencil line (B). With a bit of the same size as the thread escutcheon bore a hole right through the stile. Place the escutcheon over the hole, perfectly upright, and tap with the hammer to make an indentation on the wood. Saw down the sides of the straight part with a keyhole-saw (C) and chisel away the waste. The escutcheon can then be hammered down flush, the final tap being made over a block of hardwood.

To mark the position of the body of the lock, fix the door stile in the vice,

Fig. 10 (*opposite*). STAGES IN RECESSING HINGES

and, holding the lock with the pin level with the pencil line, mark the extent of the lock body (D). With the gauge mark the depth and width of the lock. Saw across the grain at the ends and at one or two intermediate positions to break up the grain. The saw can only be taken down as far as the diagonal (E). The depth, of course, is that of the lock body including the plate. Chisel away the waste by part chopping, part paring.

By placing the lock in position the extent of the sides of the top and back plates can be marked with a marking-knife at the ends. The edges parallel with the wood can be gauged, but as the recess makes it awkward to do this, the gauge can be set to the lock plate width plus a piece of, say, $\frac{1}{4}$ in. wood as at (F). By placing the same piece of wood on the door the gauge can freely be used (G). Both width and depth can be gauged in the same way. Again remove the waste by sawing and chiselling (H), and screw on the lock.

To find the position of the bolt-hole in the cabinet, the top of the bolt is smeared with anything that will mark—old dirty oil from the oilstone, paint,

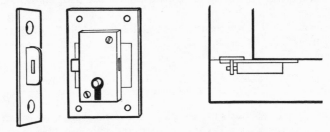

Fig. 11. LINK PLATE LOCK AND HOW FITTED

etc. The door is closed and the key turned as far as it will go, so leaving a mark on the wood. The recess is chopped with a small chisel.

A drawer lock is fitted in exactly the same way, except of course that the keyhole is at right angles with the edge. Some locks are made with two holes at the pin at right angles with each other so that they can be used for either a door or a drawer.

Link Plate Lock

When a door has to close over the cabinet ends rather than be contained between them the ordinary cut lock is clearly useless. A special type having a link-plate is required, the latter being screwed to the cabinet end. It is shown in Fig. 11. To fit this the lock is let into the back of the door first, its position in from the edge being fixed by the link-plate. Having been cut in and screwed in position, the link-plate is attached to the back and the door pushed home as far as it will go. Many link plates have two small spikes at the back which become indented in the wood, so fixing the position. This enables the edges to be marked and the recess cut. Incidentally, in some such locks the bolt swings out at either side, enabling the lock to be used right or left hand. In this case a recess to take the bolt must be cut.

Box locks are similar in that a link plate is needed. Fitting is similar.

Bolts and Catches

Ordinary screw-on bolts call for no special explanation. Cut bolts are rather more awkward. Having decided on the position (if on an edge it is central) a recess is cut to take the bolt and other projecting parts. This enables the bolt to be held in position and a mark made around the plate. This is then recessed, the ends being made longer by the thickness of the plate itself.

Ball catches usually need nothing more than a hole to receive the cylindrical body of the bolt, though some larger catches have a plate at the top which needs to be recessed. A recess to receive the catch-plate is generally needed. This plate is usually bent over slightly to enable the ball to function easily. Some workers prefer to fit the bolt to the carcase and the plate to the door as the whole is then entirely invisible from the front. When the wood is thin, however, this may not be practicable.

Knock-down Fittings

These are largely used in the trade and have the advantage that pieces of furniture can be stacked flat. Storage space is thus saved and the cost of transport cut down since far less van accommodation is needed. Many of them work on a cam system which has the effect of drawing the parts tightly together. Others have a wedge action, and there is also a bolt and fly nut type for holding legs to rails.

10 Wood Finishing

THE CHOICE OF finish depends upon the job itself. Outdoor work is generally painted or, in the case of decorative hardwoods, varnished. Indoor work if in softwood is usually painted, too, especially when such materials as hardboard and plywood are used with it. Most hardwoods when used for furniture, fitments, or small items are polished as a rule. They may also be stained first. Some sort of finish is generally desirable because, apart from enhancing the appearance, it seals the grain and helps in avoiding movement due to humidity changes in the atmosphere. The chief kinds of finish are wax, french polish, cellulose lacquer, catalyst polish, varnish, and various special polishes such as table-top polish; or there may be a combination of certain of them.

Wax Polish

This is the easiest to apply and may be renewed at any time. It gives an attractive eggshell gloss and has little darkening effect on the wood beyond the slight deepening that all finishes give (even clear water makes the wood look darker). On the other hand, it does not keep out dirt well, and items liable to be handled much can soon become dirty in appearance. This, however, can be avoided by giving one or two preliminary coats of french polish or diluted cellulose lacquer. This gives a basic shine and helps to keep out dirt.

Either proprietary polish can be used, or it can be made from beeswax and turps. It is put on with a brush of the boot-brush type and allowed to wait until the turps has evaporated (no shine can be built up until this happens). The surface is burnished with another brush and finished off with a cloth. One word of warning when an oil stain has previously been used. It is essential that this is fixed with french polish or a coat of sealer, otherwise the turps in the wax polish will lift the stain in patches.

French Polish

This is the traditional finish for cabinet work and has many advantages, amongst them being the fact that the shine it gives appears as a burnish of the wood itself, whereas many modern polishes look like a coating on the surface. On the other hand, it does not resist heat, water, and spirit marking, and is thus not ideal for a table-top unless the table is carefully used. Furthermore, it takes practice to get a really good result.

There are several varieties of french polish, the chief being: *garnet*, a dark polish used chiefly when the tone has to be deepened; *orange*, a medium brown polish, again tending to deepen and warm the colour; *button*, a yellowish polish which has the reputation of being harder than the others but is slightly milky. It should never be used over orange or garnet, always before; *white*, a milky white polish used on light woods; and *transparent*, a slightly yellow but transparent polish, again used on light woods.

As it is usually required to build up a perfectly flat surface, the grain is usually filled in first, though some coarse woods like oak are often left unfilled. Various fillers can be used. Perhaps the commonest, and one widely used in the trade, is plaster of Paris. The procedure is first to give two rubbers of french polish, the purpose of which is to seal any stain that may have been applied, and to prevent the later absorption of oil into the pores and thus avoiding the filler turning white in the grain.

The plaster is shaken out into a little pile and dry pigment added to take off the whiteness. This may be red ochre for mahogany and similar coloured woods and burnt umber for dark oak. A coarse rag is dampened with water, dipped into the mixture, and applied to the surface with a circular movement. After a short while the damp appearance will go off, and the surface is then rubbed across the grain. Remember that the purpose is solely to fill in the open pores, not to put on a surface coating. Allow to dry out thoroughly when the appearance will be that of a rather dirty white smear. Now dip a rag into linseed oil and go over the entire surface. This will kill any remaining whiteness, and enable any surplus to be wiped off as a scum. Again leave several hours to dry out.

French polishing now begins. Make a rubber from unbleached cotton wool moulded into a sort of pear shape, and shake french polish on to it until firm pressure causes a little to exude. It must not be anywhere near dripping wet. Cut a piece of linen, or any soft material free from fluff, to about 8 in. square, place the cotton-wool about 1 in. from the front edge and fold the edges to form an egg shape. Press the rubber on to a flat surface so that the sole is flat and free from all creases, and it is ready for use. Whenever further polish is needed the cover should always be removed first.

The first rubber or two should be applied without any oil, but afterwards it is necessary to lubricate the sole with a spot of linseed oil. Do not overdo the oil, however, because it all has to be got rid of later. Use the rubber with a circular movement, starting at one edge and working gradually across the entire surface. Recharge with polish when necessary, but work the rubber out. In all circumstances avoid overcharging because it will otherwise leave ridges of polish which have to be got rid of. In any case it is not the quantity of polish that gives the shine, but rather the friction of the rubber over the half-hard shellac.

To spread the polish, the movement of the rubber can be changed to a figure-of-eight movement, and finally to long back and forth strokes *with* the grain. On no account begin or end the movement by abruptly placing the rubber on the surface. Rather glide it on and off. Continue this bodying process until a good depth of polish has been built up. The last movement should be in long strokes with the grain, the polish thinned with about 50 per cent methylated spirit.

There are various ways of finishing off, but probably the simplest is that known as spiriting. A fresh rubber should be prepared and the cotton-wool given one or two drops of spirit, no more. It should not even feel damp when touched. Flatten in a board, and go over the surface in long strokes, so gradually removing the oil and building up a bright sheen. Shift the cover to a fresh part as it becomes greasy, and increase the pressure as it dries out. At all costs avoid a damp rubber.

Heat Resistant Polishes

These have their obvious advantages for table tops, etc. Some are applied in precisely the same way as french polish except that no oil must be used. Thus it is impossible to use plaster of Paris because this involves the use of oil, apart from its use as a lubricant. In this case a paste filler such as Wheeler's compound is needed.

Most heat-resistant polishes, however, are of the catalyst type, in which the hardening agent is added immediately before use. It then has a limited working life after which it becomes useless. Some are purely for brush application; others can be used with the rubber. Generally it is essential to avoid the use of oil stains beforehand.

Cellulose Lacquer

These are almost entirely for spray application, except for quite small work. The point about them is that the liquid part is so extremely volatile that it is impossible to go over a large surface without join marks showing. Some woods, such as sycamore, tend to lose their colour on exposure, but a special polish which absorbs ultra-violet light is available which prevents this.

Oil Polish

This gives an attractive finish. It has an eggshell gloss and is resistant to heat, water, and spirit-marking, and can be renewed or revived at any time. On the other hand, it takes a long time. Linseed oil is used with a small quantity of driers added. The latter could be terebene or *Universal Medium*. The latter is a form of varnish, and has the advantage of adding to the shine.

Apply the oil with a rag. The latter should exude oil when pressed but should not be dripping wet. Rub vigorously with a circular movement and leave to dry out. Many applications are needed to build up any degree of shine. It is the rubbing with frequent drying intervals that gives the finish, not the quantity of oil applied.

STAINING

Some prefer to colour the wood before polishing. There are many proprietary stains, and they may be oil, water, or spirit based. Generally water stains are cheaper but are inclined to raise the grain. Consequently before a water stain is used the wood should be dampened with warm water and allowed to dry out. It is then glasspapered afresh. Subsequent staining will not be so liable to raise the grain.

In the trade a standard water stain for oak is Vandyke crystals dissolved in water with a little ammonia added immediately before use. It gives a rather cold brown stain, light or dark according to strength. The ammonia has an additional darkening effect, but, more important, it drives the stain into the grain. If necessary the colour can be warmed by adding a very little eosin powder colour (made up separately in water).

Mahogany is darkened with bichromate of potash crystals steeped in water to make a saturated solution. It turns the water a bright orange colour, but its effect on the wood is to darken it chemically to a brown colour which can be almost black if really strong. It darkens some other woods such as walnut and to an extent oak, but leaves some woods unchanged.

Other stains can be made with aniline dyes which are obtainable in powder form, and need mixing with water, spirit, or oil according to type. Many of the colours are rather unorthodox for wood, however, being bright reds, greens, yellow, etc., and require using with care. Proprietary ready-made stains are available in a wide range of colours and either ready mixed in liquid form, or in powder to which the appropriate liquid is added.

The order of procedure in a job to be french polished is as follows: the wood is cleaned up thoroughly by planing, scraping, and glasspapering. If water stain is to be used the entire surface is dampened with warm water, and glasspapered afresh. Staining follows, again with a drying interval. Two coats of french polish are given, and the grain filled in. If this is plaster of Paris (see page 148) a rubbing with linseed oil follows, and the bodying process begins, ending with the finishing process. In all these stages it is most important to allow each to dry out or harden before the next follows. This usually means 12–24 hours, depending upon the atmosphere, temperature, and the particular operation.

11 Drawing

THIS IS AN essential part of woodwork. Any job of any importance needs it, either to enable the proportions to be judged, the construction to be worked out, or the accommodation and general practicability to be ascertained. The types of drawing needed are usually a preliminary freehand sketch in which the main idea (often with several alternatives) is roughed in, followed by a scale drawing in which the same ideas are brought to a more exact form, and finally a full-size drawing in which details are finalized. In quite small jobs

Fig. 1. IDEAS ROUGHLY SKETCHED IN PENCIL

the scale drawing is usually omitted, but the full sizing is invariably needed except for the simplest of jobs.

After the rough sketch (Fig. 1) the scale drawing enables the accommodation and proportions to be decided, and usual scales are 1 in., 1½ in., and 2 in. to the foot, though when the item is small a 3 in. scale has its advantages. The ordinary rule can be used for 1½ in. and 3 in. scales, since in the former the eighths represent inches, and the quarters in the other. This scale drawing (Fig. 2) is quickly prepared and it brings to light any main discrepancies which can be put right, but it frequently happens that still further alteration have to be made in the full-size drawing. Indeed it is only in the latter that the thing can be finalized.

This drawing can be made on detail paper (or any other conveniently large sheet) or on ply or hardboard. Sometimes only part of the job need be drawn—say, one half. In any case it is desirable to put the ground line right at the bottom edge because then the whole thing can be placed on the floor against the wall in the position it will occupy. It is only in this way that the proportions can be properly judged.

Fig. 2. SCALE ELEVATIONS SHOWING PROPORTIONS

When satisfied with the proportions various sections can be put in to enable construction to be worked out or shapes drawn in. Quite often only a side section is needed. Sometimes not even the whole of this is needed. For instance, in a deep job the front and back are drawn in at any convenient distance apart, the actual size marked in, and broken lines put in to show that the lines put in are not the actual size as shown at (B), Fig. 3. In another way a side section is often superimposed upon the front elevation, again with broken lines. Depending upon the job, a plan may be needed, especially if the job has a broken front with one part deeper than another, or if there are shapes such as in a bow-front cabinet. It is, in fact, a case of taking the job on its merits and deciding exactly what is essential. Any detail that will make the construction obvious can be added. In the case of a trade job there is no need

153

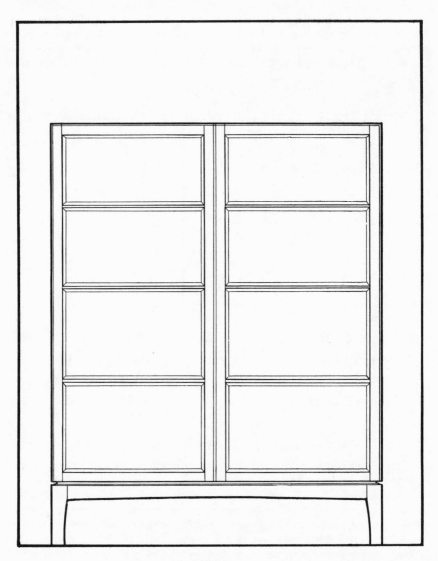

Fig. 3. A. FULL-SIZE DRAWING ON PAPER OR PLYWOOD
The purpose of this is solely to enable proportions and accommodation to be judged

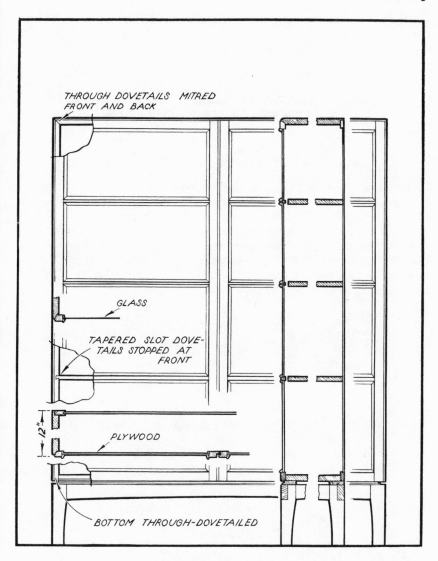

THROUGH DOVETAILS MITRED
FRONT AND BACK

GLASS

TAPERED SLOT DOVE-
TAILS STOPPED AT
FRONT

12"

PLYWOOD

BOTTOM THROUGH-DOVETAILED

Fig. 3. B. FULL-SIZE DRAWING WITH SECTIONS ADDED
The last named show the sections to be followed. If broken lines are put in the
dimensions should be written in

to draw in all joints in detail. These can be left to the maker unless for any special reason a certain construction is required (it may, for instance, be necessary to work to a price or resist a special stress).

Fig. 4. RADIUS STICK FOR LARGE CURVES

When the full-size drawing is required solely to enable proportions, etc., to be decided it is desirable to put in the job completely, because it is only in this way that the effect can be ascertained. Many shapes have to be drawn freehand, but circular curves should be put in either with compasses or by a radius stick which centres upon a nail and has notches in various positions to suit the radius of the circle (Fig. 4). Regular shapes, such as the ellipse, should be drawn by the pin and string method (Fig. 5). Never attempt to use the compass method as it gives an ugly shape.

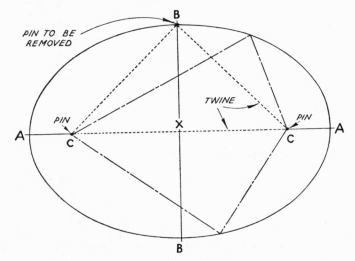

Fig. 5. SETTING OUT ELLIPSE, THREAD AND PIN METHOD

Set out two axes AA and BB at right angles to and bisecting each other. Take half the length of AA (that is XA) and with divider leg at (B) mark points (CC) on the longer axis. Tap in fine pins at B. C. C, and around all three tie a length of fine thread. Remove pin at (B). By taking a sharp pointed pencil and using the loose thread as a trammel a correct ellipse of the required size may be drawn.

DESIGNS SECTION

Tray

HAVING A PLASTIC surface, this tray does not become marked in use and is not damaged by hot water or spirit marks. Furthermore, the section of the edging enables it to be cleaned easily since the hollow section finishes level with the surface of the plastic (see Fig. 2). A close-grained hardwood is used for the handles. They can be either in a contrasting wood or they can match.

Plywood $\frac{1}{2}$ in. thick is used for the main panel, and the first step, having squared it, is to put down the plastic sheet with a contact adhesive. As the panel has a shallow rebate all round and the plastic sheet finishes level with this, the method of working calls for some consideration since it depends upon the facilities available. Those who have a portable electric router or have access to a spindle moulder will have no difficulty. The sheet is cut about $\frac{1}{8}$ in. oversize in each direction, and the plywood panel is gauged round to the extent of the rebate. The sheet is laid in position so that it just overlaps the gauge line all round, and three panel pins are tapped in at one end as shown in Fig. 3, also a single pin at one side. Having applied the contact adhesive to both ply

Fig. 1. EASY-CLEAN TRAY WITH PLASTIC FACING

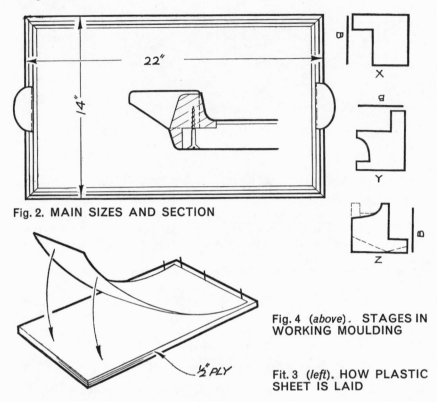

Fig. 2. MAIN SIZES AND SECTION

Fig. 4 (*above*). STAGES IN WORKING MOULDING

Fit. 3 (*left*). HOW PLASTIC SHEET IS LAID

and sheet, and left a while as given in the instructions, the sheet is bent, held against the pins, and pressed down. This method gives exact position and avoids trapping air at the joining surfaces.

It is now a case of cutting the rebate, using the rebating cutter in the router. Generally, it is more satisfactory to fit the router beneath a working table and run the panel along the cutter. It will be realized that there is only the merest skim of plastic to be removed.

If hand methods have to be used, it is better to work the rebate all round the panel first and trim the plastic sheet so that it is a trifle full all round. It is then laid in the way already described, the pins being driven in at the edge of the rebate. This will leave only a slight shaving to be taken from the plastic panel, the shoulder or bullnose plane being used.

When the moulding can be made on the electric router or spindle moulder, the stages in Fig. 4 are advisable. At (X) the rebate is worked. Note the wide uncut surface which rests on the machining table. Next, the hollow is cut (Y), an uncut portion being left so that there is ample bearing surface on the table. Lastly, the tongue of wood is removed and the wood planed to a slight slope by hand (Z). The outer chamfers can be planed after the moulding has been fixed.

If the moulding has to be worked by hand, the rebate is cut first and the wood gripped in the vice by the projecting lip. This enables a preliminary chamfer to be worked before the hollow is planed.

Mitre the moulding round and fix with screws from beneath. Each side is then released, the joining surfaces glued and the screws driven in afresh. It is, of course, easier to polish the moulding in a length before mitring and fixing.

Cut notches in the moulding to receive the handles and fix with screws. To give a neat finish, the underside of the tray can be lined.

Bread Trays

THESE TRAYS CAN be made in any hardwood, and when fitted with coloured or decorated tiles make delightful tableware which can be used for bread, sweets, biscuits, etc.

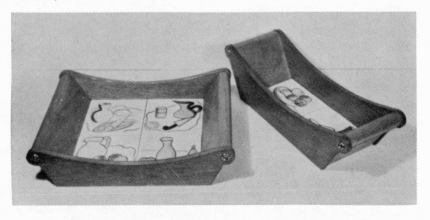

Fig. 1. SMALL ITEMS WHICH MAKE EXCELLENT GIFTS

Design Section

The trays shown in Fig. 1 are made to take decorated tiles measuring $4\frac{1}{4}$ in. square, but the design can be easily adapted to fit any particular size of tile required.

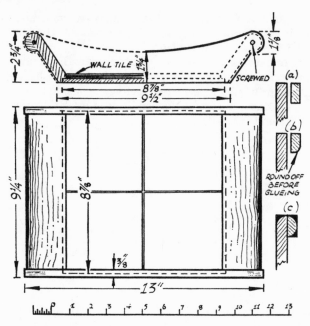

Fig. 2. ELEVATION AND PLAN OF LARGE TRAY WITH DETAILS

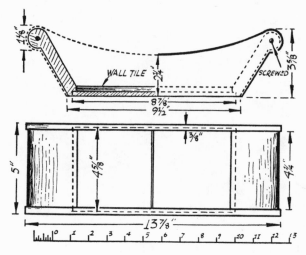

Fig. 3. SIZES OF SMALL TRAY

The End Sections

These are made of $\frac{5}{8}$ in. wood. The rounded top edges are built up by gluing strips $\frac{7}{8}$ in. by $\frac{1}{4}$ in. along the top edges. They are cramped down until the glue has set. The rounded shape can be planed and finished with glasspaper, first Middle 2 then No. 1. This detail is given at (*a*), (*b*), and (*c*), Fig. 2. It is a help if the bottom edge of the strip is rounded before gluing.

The bottom edges are rebated $\frac{3}{16}$ in. to take the base plywood panel. The angle of the rebate must, of course, be appropriate to the angle of the slope of the ends. If the shape of the side panels is drawn on card to the measurements in Fig. 2 it will give the correct angle for the ends. Note that the inside edges are at an angle to enable the tiles to fit neatly. The angle will agree with that of the rebate.

Side Panels

These are of $\frac{3}{8}$ in. wood. The ends are cut to the required shape including the rounded top. The latter is $1\frac{1}{8}$ in. diameter and so protrudes $\frac{1}{8}$ in. beyond the ends, as shown by dotted line in Figs. 2 and 3. The top curve can be drawn with compasses set to $7\frac{1}{4}$ in. radius, or it can be sketched in by hand, following a long sweeping curve. Alternatively, a narrow strip of wood can be bent to shape, and a pencil run along the edge. The bottom edges are rebated $\frac{3}{16}$ in. to accommodate the plywood base. These rebates can be stopped $\frac{5}{16}$ in. from the ends or carried straight through and filled later.

The Bottom

This is of $\frac{1}{4}$ in. ply cut to the necessary measurements. The tiles are ordinary wall type, either plain, coloured, or decorated to the individual choice.

(Continued on next page)

Cutting List

						Long ft. in.	Wide in.	Thick in.
Small Tray								
2 Ends	..	..	..	..	..	5	$4\frac{1}{2}$	$\frac{5}{8}$
2 Edgings	..	..	..	..	..	5	1	$\frac{1}{4}$
2 Sides	..	..	..	..	1	$2\frac{1}{4}$	$3\frac{3}{4}$	$\frac{3}{8}$
1 Bottom	..	..	..	..		$9\frac{1}{4}$	$4\frac{7}{8}$	$\frac{1}{4}$
Large Tray								
2 Ends	..	..	..	..	..	$9\frac{1}{4}$	$3\frac{1}{2}$	$\frac{5}{8}$
2 Edgings	..	..	..	..	..	$9\frac{1}{4}$	1	$\frac{1}{4}$
2 Sides	..	..	..	..	1	$1\frac{1}{2}$	3	$\frac{3}{8}$
1 Bottom	..	..	..	..		$9\frac{1}{4}$	$9\frac{1}{4}$	$\frac{1}{4}$

Allowance has been made in lengths and widths. Thicknesses are net.

Before assembling, all parts (other than joints) should be given two coats of french polish.

Assembling

The side panels are glued and screwed to the ends at the top. The sides are drilled to take $\frac{3}{4}$ in. No. 6 brass screws and cups. These, apart from strengthening the joint, add to the appearance of the trays. When the joints have thoroughly set the bottom is glued and either screwed or pinned into the ends. When the glue has set, the joints can be cleaned, after which the finishing coats of french polish can be given, avoiding the inside of the bottom to which the wall tiles are affixed with *Evo-stick* after polishing has been finished and dried.

Stool and Workbox

STANDARD PRACTICE IS used in making the stool.

Sides

Set out and cut partition housings, and rebate top and bottom edges to take lid and base. Mark out the positions of flutes in pencil, and clamp on a straight-edge. Using this as a fence, plane out the groove with a No. 8 round plane until required depth is reached. Repeat the procedure for each flute. Finally mark out the tenons.

Legs

Make up a template for the freehand curve and mark out the legs to leave a $\frac{3}{4}$ in. square foot. When completed shape the inside edges, remove the top inner corner (A), Fig. 3, and cut the mortises and tenons. At this stage the frame is cleaned up and glued together. When set, mark the curve and outer chamfer (B), Fig. 2. The line of the chamfer is parallel with the shaping. Note from Figs. 1 and 2 how the combined effect is to produce the illusion of a shaped leg, whereas in reality the outer line is straight when seen in elevation.

Glue in the partitions and pin where necessary; also base and fillets. Complete the framework by working the chamfer around the top edge.

Tray

This is dovetailed at the corners, the centre section being stopped housed. The base is glued and pinned in place (see Fig. 4). Top outer edges can be rounded, chamfered, or left square.

Top

The thickness of upholstery, if taken round the edges, governs the size of the top, and this must be taken into account when shaping.

Fig. 1. USEFUL DUAL-PURPOSE ITEM

Upholstery

Tack on to the top surface a piece of hessian stuffed with wood wool or some other suitable material. Over this padding is placed the final covering. If the interlaced leather top is desired, as shown in Fig. 1, cut the leather into strips of approximately 1 in. wide and 18 in. long, interlacing them over the padding and pinning to the underside of the lid. The inside surface is padded in a similar manner to take pins, needles, etc. The tacks are covered by a narrow gimp or braid.

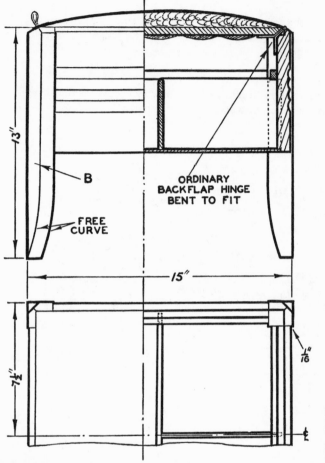

Fig. 2.
ELEVATION
WITH PART
SECTION AND
PLAN

Hingeing

Leather hinges or back-flaps are used to fix the top. If back-flaps are decided on, these are bent as shown in Fig. 5, the measurement (X) being the diagonal distance formed by rebate (see exploded view, Fig. 3). When fixing the hinge to the lid, it is recessed as shown at (C), Fig. 3. To prevent the seat falling too far back when opened, a short chain or stay is fitted, length and type of which is left to individual taste.

Finish

The completed stool is finished in clear polish or stained to blend with existing furniture.

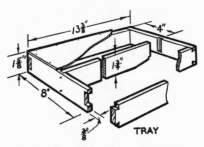

Fig. 4. HOW TRAY IS MADE

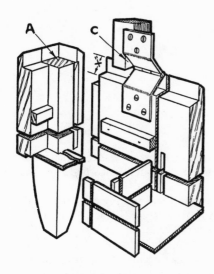

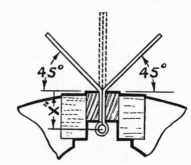

Fig. 3. EXPLODED VIEW OF
CONSTRUCTION
Fig. 5. (*right*). METHOD OF BENDING
HINGE

Cutting List
Stool

					Long ft.	in.	Wide in.	Thick in.
4 Legs	..	..	..	..	I	$1\frac{1}{2}$	$1\frac{1}{2}$	$1\frac{3}{8}$
4 Sides	..	..	..	..	I	2	$7\frac{1}{4}$	$\frac{3}{4}$
I Bottom	..	..	..	..	I	2	14	3 mm. ply
I Partition	..	..	..	..	I	2	$4\frac{1}{4}$	4 mm. ply
I Part	..	..	..	..		7	$4\frac{1}{4}$	4 mm. ply
I Top	..	..	..	..	I	$2\frac{1}{2}$	$14\frac{1}{2}$	$\frac{3}{8}$ or ply
Fillets	..	..	..	..	2	6	$\frac{3}{8}$	$\frac{1}{2}$

Tray

2 Sides	..	..	..	..	I	2	$1\frac{3}{4}$	$\frac{3}{8}$
2 Ends	..	..	..	..		$8\frac{1}{2}$	$1\frac{3}{4}$	$\frac{3}{8}$
I Centre	..	..	..	..	I	$1\frac{1}{2}$	2	$\frac{3}{8}$
I Bottom	..	..	..	..	I	2	$8\frac{1}{2}$	3 mm. ply

Lengths and widths allow for jointing and trimming. Thicknesses are net.

165

Tea Trolley

THE CLEAN LINES of this trolley give it an attractive appearance enhanced by the two-tone effect of the trays being veneered in a different wood from that of the framework.

In the original the frame was made of rauli and the plywood trays were veneered with white limba finished with heat-resisting lacquer. If preferred, however, the trays could be made of thinner plywood, say, $\frac{5}{16}$ in., and overlaid with a patterned plastic laminate. If the latter method is adopted, means must be found to hold the plywood flat while the plastic laminate is being glued to it; gluing the laminate to one side of the ply only tends to curl the latter.

Fig. 1. TROLLEY IN RAULI WITH WHITE LIMBA TRAYS

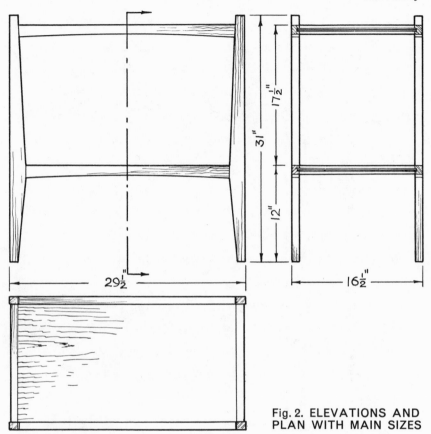

Fig. 2. ELEVATIONS AND
PLAN WITH MAIN SIZES

The Frame

This is made from $\frac{7}{8}$ in. thick material throughout. The side frames should be made up first to the shape shown in Fig. 2. Set out on a sheet of hardboard a full-size drawing of one leg to the dimensions given in Fig. 3, showing the rail positions, etc. This drawing will enable the bevels for the shoulders of the top rails to be obtained.

Next, prepare four legs to finish 31 in. long by 2 in. wide, and four side rails 29 in. long by $1\frac{1}{2}$ in. wide. Taper the legs on the inside faces to the dimensions given in Fig. 2. The joints between the side rails and legs can now be cut. Notice from Fig. 3 that the mortises and tenons are set back $\frac{1}{8}$ in. at the ends. Fit these frames together and test in cramps to see that the joints fit and that the frames pull up square.

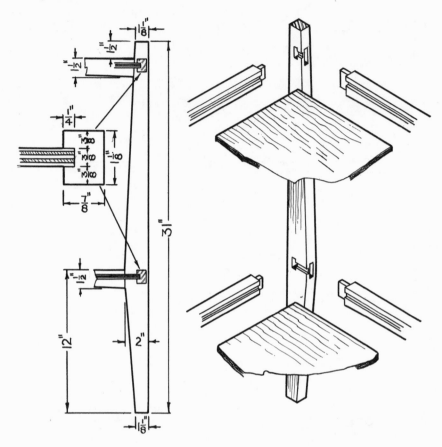

Fig. 3. SECTION AT END   Fig. 4. EXPLODED VIEW

End Rails

Prepare four of these 16 in. long by $1\frac{1}{8}$ in. wide and fit them to the legs with mortise and tenon joints, as in Fig. 4. The rails should be set in from the outside edges of the legs $\frac{1}{8}$ in. and their top edges should be aligned with the top edges of the side rails.

The Trays

Prepare two pieces of 9 mm. plywood each 28 in. by $15\frac{1}{4}$ in. Veneer the top face of each with any chosen wood. Clean up the veneered surfaces and finish them with heat-resisting lacquer. Having finished the trays the exact size of the plough cutter required to make the grooves along the rails to receive the trays can be measured. If a cutter exactly right is not available, choose the nearest, but less than the thickness of the tray material, and rebate round the under edges of the trays to suit the grooves made by the cutter.

Next, groove the rails to receive the trays. As will be seen in the detail drawing in Fig. 3, the grooves should be $\frac{3}{8}$ in. down from the top edges of the rails and $\frac{1}{4}$ in. deep.

Gluing the Side Frames

The side rails are curved on their lower edges. Each curve rises $\frac{3}{8}$ in. at the centre. These curves should next be shaped.

The side frames can now be glued together and set square. When the glue has set, clean up the faces of the frames and extend the grooves through the legs to meet the mortises of the end rails, as shown in Fig. 4.

Final Fitting and Assembly

The whole structure, including the trays, may now be temporarily assembled to make sure that every part fits. After knocking apart, it would be wise to polish end rails and side frames before re-assembly.

Cutting List

					Long ft.	Long in.	Wide in.	Thick in.
4 Legs	..	..	..	..	2	$7\frac{1}{2}$	$2\frac{1}{4}$	$\frac{7}{8}$
4 Side rails	..	..	..	..	2	$5\frac{1}{2}$	$1\frac{3}{4}$	$\frac{7}{8}$
4 End rails	..	..	..	..	1	$4\frac{1}{2}$	$1\frac{3}{8}$	$\frac{7}{8}$
2 Trays	..	..	..	..	2	$4\frac{1}{4}$	$15\frac{3}{8}$	9 mm.
2 Sheets of veneer		..	..	..	2	$4\frac{1}{4}$	$15\frac{3}{8}$	
4 Castors								

Allowances have been made in lengths and widths; thicknesses are net.

Occasional Table

A SIZE OF 30 in. by about 14 in. makes this table suitable for afternoon tea or evening coffee. Its light weight enables it to be moved about easily, and the plastic top makes cleaning simple.

Main sizes are given in Fig. 2. They could be varied within a little to suit any special sizes of material that may be available.

Construction is simple, consisting of plain mortise-and-tenon joints for the stand, and a panel of blockboard, multi-ply, or chipboard for the top

Fig. 1. LIGHT TABLE WITH PLASTIC FACING

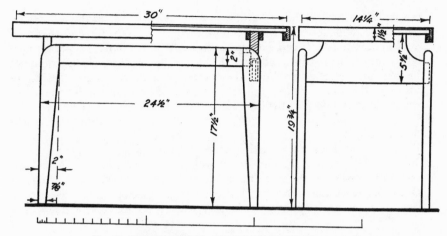

Fig. 2. ELEVATIONS. NOTE PLOTTING OF JOINTS

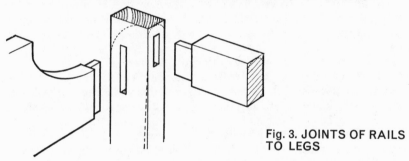

Fig. 3. JOINTS OF RAILS TO LEGS

covered with plastic material. The latter in Fig. 1 is in three pieces, but it could be in a single piece if preferred, or made up to a design using several small pieces. The latter has the advantage of using oddments and is usually cheaper. It is, of course, important that all are of the same thickness because levelling is impossible afterwards.

Stand

It is advisable to set out one corner of this in full size so that the positions of the various details are obvious. As the corner of the leg is cut to a curve it is necessary to plot the extent of the tenon so that it is well within the shape. This has also to be considered in relation to the end rail which has to be set down so that its top edge is contained within the curve.

The legs can either be prepared in parallel strips and the taper sawn or planed after the mortises have been cut, or they can be marked out in tapered form, this having the advantage of making an economy in material. Note that

171

the taper starts beneath the top rail so that the shoulders of the rail can be cut square. Whichever method is followed the curve at the top corner should not be cut until later because otherwise it would be awkward to apply cramps. The same applies to the rounding of the top and outer edges, which should not be done until after assembling. The end rails can be shaped in their entirety beforehand because without this tenoning would be awkward. The mortises should be cut as deep as the limited thickness of the wood will allow.

Assembling

Front and back frames are glued up independently. When the glue has set the joints are levelled and the top corners rounded. Lastly, the top edge of each rail is rounded over, the rounding continuing across the legs, and dying out as it proceeds around the curve. The end rails are glued in next. Take care to clean away all surplus glue before it sets because it is impossible to do so later.

Top

Use ½ in. multi-ply, blockboard, or chipboard for this. Trim to size and pre-pare the plastic material for the facing. It is best put down with a caul. Put the three sheets of plastic together in position on the bench, and put a strip of gummed tape over each joint. Use cold setting resin glue. Press down with a flat caul, and damp and peel away the gummed tape afterwards.

To the underside all round is fixed a framework of 1 in. by ½ in. stuff. The corners are dovetailed in the best work, or butted and glued and nailed for a cheaper job. The panel is glued down on to it, and the edges levelled after the glue has set. Lastly, the edging proper is mitred round. Glue alone will hold it if carefully done, otherwise it can also be pinned, the nails being punched in and the holes filled. To hold the top in position corner fillets of wood are glued and rubbed in. Alternatively, square blocks could be used, these being screwed into both top and end rails.

Cutting List

					Long ft.	in.	Wide in.	Thick in.
1 Top	..	..	..	..	..	2	6¼	14½	½
4 Legs	..	..	..	..	..	1	6½	2¼	⅞
2 Rails	..	..	..	..	..	1	10½	2¼	⅞
2 Rails	..	..	..	..	..	1	2½	5¾	⅞
2 Lippings	..	..	..	..	2	8	1¾	⅜
2 Lippings	..	..	..	..	1	3½	1¾	⅜
1 Plastic top	..	..	..	..	2	6¼	14½	—
2 Frame Rails	..	..	..	..	2	6	1¼	½
2 Frame Rails	..	..	..	..	1	2	1¼	½

Comfortable Easy Chair

With Loose Cushions

THIS CHAIR USES two moulded latex cushions, size 22 in. by 21 in. by 4 in. resting on Pirelli rubber webbing. These give a slight overhang at the front of

Fig. 1. CHAIR WITH CLEAN FLOWING LINES

the seat and at the head of the back, so ensuring comfort. The front seat rail is hollowed along the top edge so that there is appreciable give for the front of the seat cushion, and the back rail against which the back rests is also curved, again to ensure that the rubber webbing is able to give against the weight. One other point helping to make the chair comfortable is that the shaped arms are sloped inwards in section at the middle so enabling the arms to rest easily.

Oak was used for the chair in Fig. 1, but almost any good quality hardwood could be used. The legs are turned in their entirety, necessitating the special mortise and tenon joints shown in Fig. 4. The top edges of the rails are hollowed at the shoulder to enable them to fit up to the circular leg section, but the legs themselves have flats cut locally so that square shoulders can be cut across the rails. It will be realized that it would be awkward to cut hollow shoulders right across the rails. By offsetting as at (B) the tenons can be longer than if centred (A), Fig. 7.

At the top of the legs are dowels which pass right through the arms and

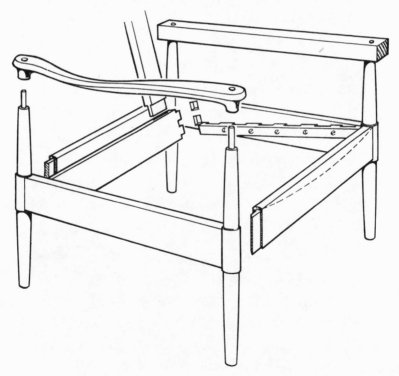

Fig. 2. GENERAL VIEW OF CONSTRUCTION

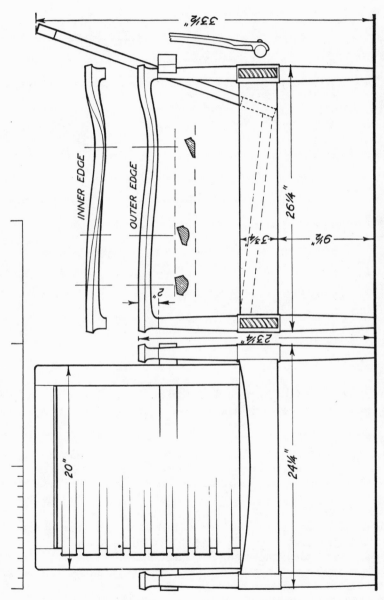

Fig. 3. FRONT AND SIDE ELEVATION. ALSO ARM SECTIONS AND BACK RAIL SHAPE

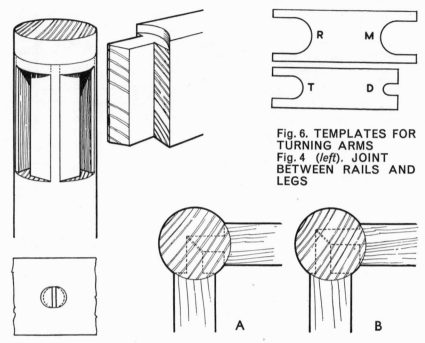

Fig. 6. TEMPLATES FOR TURNING ARMS
Fig. 4 *(left)*. JOINT BETWEEN RAILS AND LEGS

Fig. 5. HOW DOWEL IS WEDGED AT TOP

Fig. 7. LEG SECTIONS SHOWING TENONS

are wedged at the top. To enable the back to be anchored at the bottom, a sloping rail is stub-tenoned into the side seat rails (Fig. 2). The uprights are tenoned into this, and a curved rail screwed to the top of the back legs (Fig. 3) provides a bearing for the back.

Legs

These are first turned to the diameter of the portion opposite the rails ($1\frac{3}{4}$ in.), and the slight set-in and curved taper worked at each side. To ensure all being alike cut a pair of templates in plywood as in Fig. 6. These can be marked R (rail position), M (middle, above and below rail), T (top and bottom) and D (dowel).

Flats are cut at the rail positions and it is obvious that these must be at right-angles with each other. Those who have a lathe with a mortising attachment can use the rotary miller bit. The end of this will cut the flats. When the first flat is completed it is rested upon a square block of wood, thus enabling the second cut to be made dead at right-angles with it. Mortising follows, the ends being cut square afterwards.

If this apparatus is not available it is a case of careful paring with the chisel, possibly supplemented with a flat file. When chopping mortises by hand it is necessary to make a cradle on which the wood can rest.

Arms

Bore the $\frac{1}{2}$-in. holes for the dowels half-way in from each side, the marks being squared round and gauged. After fitting, the holes are gouged and filed away at a slope along the length (not the width) at the top side and are thus elongated as in Fig. 5. In this way the wedges can take effect when driven in later. Remember to make saw cuts in the dowels so that the wedges run across the grain. The cuts need only go down about 1 in.

With the legs in position, a sharp pencil is run around the curved tops, thus showing the extent to which the arms have to be cut away. The elevation shape of the arms can then be marked in, a template being used. Note that it dips sharply at the rear, resolving into a flat curve towards the front. A bandsaw is obviously first choice in cutting the shape. Failing this, the best way is to waste away the wood, making a series of saw cuts across the grain and chopping away with chisel and mallet, finishing off with spokeshave and rasp.

The top surface is taken well down at the inner edge (Fig. 3) and when this has been brought to a clean, flowing line, the underside can be hollowed out and rounded. Note that the section varies along the length (Fig. 3). The ends can be roughly rounded and shaped, but finishing is better done after assembling.

Back

To enable the back to be fixed a sloping rail is stub-tenoned into the side seat rails. This is set at the same angle as the slope of the back, and it is advisable to draw out the whole thing in full size so that the exact angle can be ascertained. Note that the back rests on a rail which is screwed behind the back legs at the top. This rail has two semi-circular notches so that it fits around the legs and is levelled at the same angle as the back slope.

Assembling

The two sides are put together first. The seat rail is put in and cramped and the arm dropped over its dowels and cramped. It is necessary to make special hollow blocks to fit over the legs so that the cramp shoes do not damage the wood. It will be found that cramps can be applied over the extreme ends of the arms to just clear the dowels. The wedges are driven in straightway, after which the cramps can be taken off.

Arm Shaping

The glue having set, the shaping of the arms can be completed. Front, back, and sloping rails follow, and when the glue has set the back uprights and rail can be added. A decision on the fixing of the rubber webbing has to be made. If a machine router is available a neat method is to make a series of slots to enable the webbing to be passed through as in Fig. 3. It is taken right round and tacked at the inner edge.

Back

A part-plan of the curved back supporting rail is given in Fig. 3. To bore the semi-circular holes, waste pieces are cramped on at one side and the point of the bit started right on the joint. Boring is half-way from each side. Since the legs taper slightly it is necessary to ease the lower side. Two counterbored screws are used at each side and the holes filled with plugs.

To take the seat webbing two sloping fillets are screwed to the seat rails. These rails have notches cut across them so that the webbing can be tucked in afterwards, taken right round and tacked on the face. All sharp edges should be taken off to avoid wear.

The whole can be finished with a few rubbers of white french polish, then waxed. When fixing the webbing a stretch of about 2 in. in 12 in. should be allowed.

Cutting List

					Long ft.	*Long* in.	*Wide* in.	*Thick* in.
4 Legs	..	..	..	..	2	1	2 in. sq.	—
2 Arms	..	..	..	..	2	4	—	2 sq.
2 Seat rails	..	..	..	..	2	2	4	$\frac{7}{8}$
2 Seat rails	..	..	..	..	2	0	4	$\frac{7}{8}$
1 Sloping rail	..	..	..	..	2	0	4	$\frac{7}{8}$
2 Fillets	..	..	..	..	1	8	1	$\frac{7}{8}$
1 Back support rail	..	..	..	2	2	—	2 sq.
2 Back uprights	..	..	..	..	2	0	$2\frac{1}{4}$	$\frac{7}{8}$
1 Back rail ..	..	..	..	..	1	7	$2\frac{1}{4}$	$\frac{7}{8}$

Working allowance has been added to lengths and widths; thicknesses are net.

Dining Table

A CLOSED SIZE of 45 in. by 36 in., opening to just over 57 in. by 36 in., is convenient for the average dining-room. Those who prefer could reduce the

Fig. 1. HANDY SIZE TABLE FOR THE SMALL ROOM

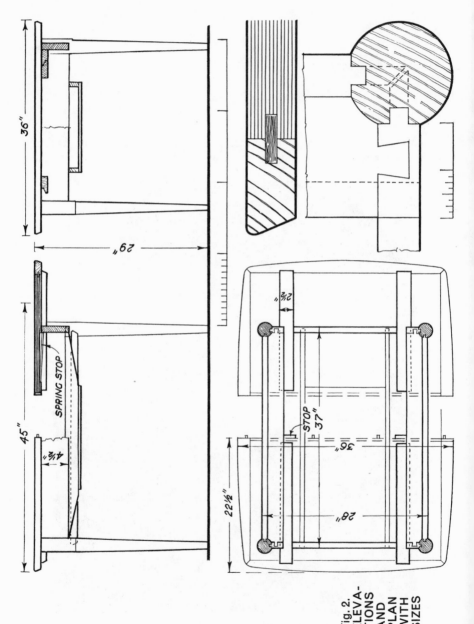

Fig. 2.
ELEVA-
TIONS
AND
PLAN
WITH
SIZES

width to 33 in. There are two sliding tops which pull out to enable a loose leaf to be dropped in.

In the table in Fig. 1 the tops are made from $\frac{3}{4}$-in. gaboon multi-ply veneered to a parquet design. It might be possible to obtain plywood parquet blocks, but the size of the table would have to be altered to suit the standard sizes of the blocks. An edging of oak is mitred round and tongued. Those who prefer could veneer both sides with plain veneer, again adding the edging.

Framework

This consists of $\frac{7}{8}$ in. rails tenoned into turned legs which finish $2\frac{1}{4}$ in. at the top. There are no squares on the legs, the rails being taken directly into the round. The simplest way of arranging the joint is to cut flats on the legs opposite the joints as in Fig. 3. Those who have a mortiser can do this accurately

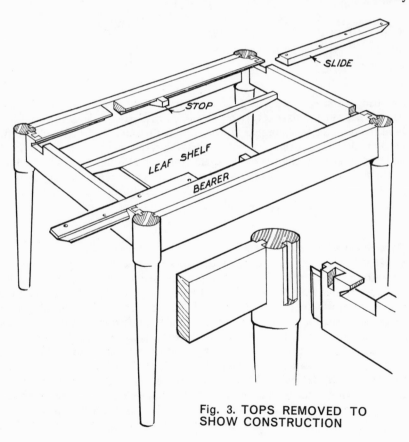

Fig. 3. TOPS REMOVED TO
SHOW CONSTRUCTION

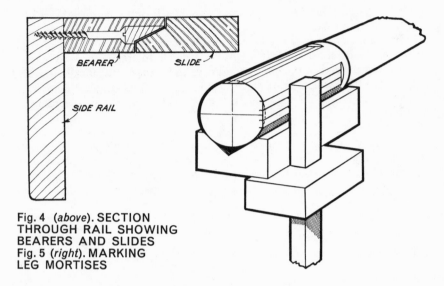

Fig. 4 (*above*). SECTION
THROUGH RAIL SHOWING
BEARERS AND SLIDES
Fig. 5 (*right*). MARKING
LEG MORTISES

by fitting a rotary miller bit. Those who have to work entirely by hand will
have to set out the flats accurately as shown in Fig. 5. A V-shaped block to
hold the rounded leg is prepared. Its width is the same as the diameter of the
leg. One diameter at the end can be marked by squaring up from the bottom,
and the other by using the gauge again from the bottom. To mark the lines
of the flats, and afterwards the mortise lines, the mortise gauge can be used.

Put two ends of the table together independently and allow the glue to set
before adding the remaining rails. The lower outer edges of the rails are
radiused.

Bearers and Slides
Rebated bearers are fixed to the framework sides, and corresponding slides
beneath the tops. Often square rebates are cut half-way in both, but it makes
a stronger job if they are sloped as in Fig. 4. Lapped dovetails are used to fix
the bearers to the end rails, the dovetails being positioned so that they clear
the rebates (see Fig. 3). Counter-bored screws are used along the length, and
it is necessary to bore the holes before the rebates are worked (see Fig. 4).

Put the dovetails in dry and mark inside the rails the line of the sloping
rebate. Square down a line giving the width of the slide, and mark in the
thickness with the gauge. Remove the waste by sawing across the grain and
chopping away with the chisel. Clearly the sloping cut must align with that
of the bearer. When nearly down to the line put in the bearer, gluing right
along the edge and screwing. Any unevenness can be levelled afterwards.

Since the slides are of the same section as the bearers they can be prepared at the same time. Each is fitted individually in its notch and numbered.

Tops

The veneering is by the caul or hammer method—unless a press is available. Front and back should be veneered simultaneously, and assuming cauls to be used, it is necessary to use several pairs of cross-bearers slightly bowed in length so that pressure is applied at the centre first, driving the glue out at the edges. Scotch glue is advisable.

The glue having set the edges should be trimmed square all round. To work the tongue grooves the most convenient method is to use the portable router with a deep fence attached so that it can be held upright without difficulty. Theoretically, the edgings are grooved with the same setting as the plywood, but in practice it is advisable to alter it slightly so that the lipping stands up a trifle proud. This enables it to be levelled afterwards.

The edging is mitred round three sides of each main top, and a $\frac{1}{2}$ in. lipping screwed on at the closing edges. In the case of the leaf only the short ends have a wide lipping. Note that the tongue groove is continued a short way along each mitre.

To level the surface a finely set smoothing plane is essential. The scraper follows, and finally glasspaper, Middle 2, $1\frac{1}{2}$, and flour. If an orbital sander is available this is ideal owing to the varying direction of the grain.

Movement of Tops

To ensure that the slides are parallel the tops are laid face down on the floor, and the framework placed in the exact position. The slides, which should be

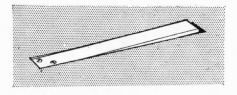

Fig. 6. SPRING STOP

free from undue friction without being slack, are placed over the tops, held close up to the bearers, and fixed with two screws each. The remaining screws are added after testing for correct running. A gap of about $1\frac{1}{4}$ in. is left between the ends of the slides, and stops are later screwed beneath the bearers as in Fig. 3. These stops ensure that the tops are about central when closed.

To prevent the tops from being pulled right out spring stops are let in beneath as in Fig. 6. Recesses to take them are cut in the tops, and one end sloped slightly so that the piece of $\frac{1}{8}$ in. hardwood which forms the spring stands up about $\frac{1}{8}$ in. It hits against the end rail when the top is pulled out. By pressing it in, however, the top can be slid right out when required. Both main tops and leaf have four dowels let in thus ensuring exact registration.

Leaf Shelf

This is a piece of plywood screwed beneath two stretchers as in Fig. 3. Notches are cut in the end rails to take the stretchers which are screwed on. There should be about $\frac{1}{4}$ in. clearance beneath the rails for the leaf.

Cutting List

	Long ft.	in.	Wide in.	Thick in.
4 Legs	2	6	$2\frac{1}{2}$ sq.	—
2 Rails	3	1	$4\frac{3}{4}$	$\frac{7}{8}$
2 Rails	2	4	$4\frac{3}{4}$	$\frac{7}{8}$
2 Bearers	3	1	$2\frac{3}{4}$	$\frac{7}{8}$
4 Slides	1	$8\frac{1}{2}$	$2\frac{3}{4}$	$\frac{7}{8}$
2 Stretchers	3	1	$2\frac{1}{2}$	$\frac{7}{8}$
1 Shelf	1	6	$15\frac{1}{4}$	$\frac{1}{4}$
2 Tops	2	$8\frac{1}{4}$	$20\frac{1}{4}$	$\frac{3}{4}$
1 Leaf	2	$8\frac{1}{4}$	$12\frac{1}{4}$	$\frac{3}{4}$
2 Edgings	3	$0\frac{1}{2}$	$2\frac{1}{4}$	$\frac{7}{8}$
4 Edgings	1	11	$2\frac{1}{4}$	$\frac{7}{8}$
2 Edgings	1	$1\frac{1}{2}$	$2\frac{1}{4}$	$\frac{7}{8}$
4 Edgings	2	9	$\frac{7}{8}$	$\frac{1}{2}$

Small parts extra.

If parquet tops are used the thickness of the edgings should be increased.

Record Cabinet

Two SEPARATE STRUCTURES are involved in making this: the cabinet proper and the stand. In addition is the special rack to hold records.

Fig. 1. CABINET WITH EXCELLENT ACCOMMODATION

Cabinet Carcase

In the best way the top is mitre-dovetailed, and the bottom lap-dovetailed to the ends. The shelf rests in grooves cut across the ends. As it is practically impossible to obtain wood wide enough for any of the parts, the first job is to glue up materials to make up the width required. Plain rubbed joints are satisfactory if well made, though those who prefer could tongue them.

Sizes are given in Fig. 2, and construction in Fig. 3. Trim the ends to the over-all shape. The bottom stands in level with the rebate for the back, and at the front finishes behind the drawer fronts. The shelf also is level with the back rebate, and the front which is chamfered and rounded) finishes just behind the moulded front edges of the ends. It is advisable to mark out the ends first, and take the shelf size from the actual job.

Mark out and cut the dovetails at top and bottom. Remember to mark an extra wide mitre at the front so that the moulding is contained within it. Fig. 3 shows the idea. The front edge of the bottom has to be planed at an angle to agree with the slope of the drawer fronts.

To hold the shelf a groove is needed, the front end being shaped to the section of the shelf. This is more satisfactory than shouldering it. Between the shelf and bottom, two uprights are needed to separate the drawers. These slope at the front. Note their positions in relation to the drawers of which the two end ones have normal dovetailed construction, whereas the centre drawer has its sides slot-dovetailed into the front. The uprights are stub-tenoned in, and grooves are cut behind them to take guides. When the ends and top have been moulded at the front and rebated at the back, and the inner surfaces cleaned up, the whole is ready for assembly.

Cramp the shelf between the ends, insert the short uprights, and add the bottom. The top can then be glued and, if necessary, cramped to bring the mitres closely together. Test for squareness before setting aside.

Drawers

The drawer guides are glued in their grooves at the front only. Construction of the three drawers is given in Fig. 4. Note that the front ends of all six sides must be at the same angle as the slope of the front. Since the fronts cloak the carcase bottom, they must be wider than the sides, and both top and bottom edges must be at an angle. As the middle drawer has slot-dovetails the length of the sides is somewhat less.

Some care is necessary to cut the dovetail slots of the middle drawer in the right positions because it is difficult to reduce them for fitting once the drawer is together. One good method is to cut the front full in length (about $\frac{1}{16}$ in.). The back is then fitted exactly to the opening, and this placed against the inside face of the front and held equidistantly in from each end. A line scribed at each end gives the position of the sides. No handles are fitted, but the inside of each front is scooped out at the bottom to provide a grip.

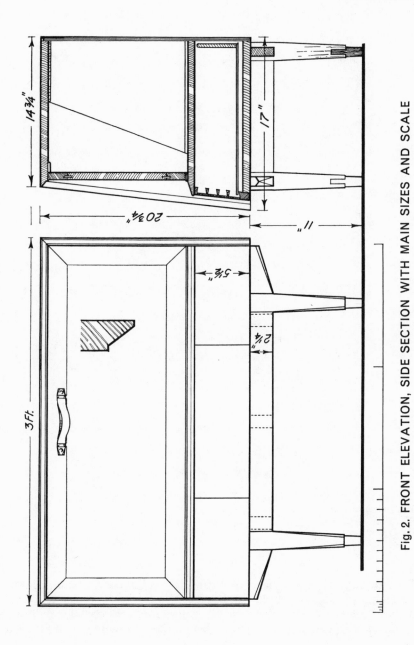

Fig. 2. FRONT ELEVATION, SIDE SECTION WITH MAIN SIZES AND SCALE

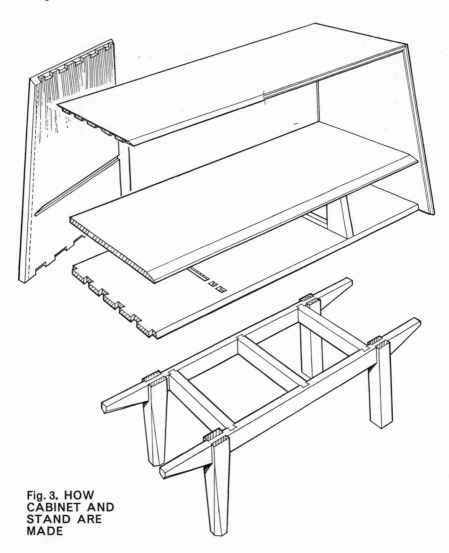

Fig. 3. HOW
CABINET AND
STAND ARE
MADE

Fall

There are various ways of making this. In Fig. 2 it was clamped with mitred and tongued joints. The wood was brought to a low moisture content, and had been indoors in stick for some ten years. This construction would be dangerous with not fully seasoned timber, probably resulting in splits. An alternative is to use blockboard or multi-ply and veneer both sides, the two being treated in one operation. In any case the fall should be lipped first, to make the edges presentable, and to provide a good hold for the hinge screws. A slip is fitted to the carcase at the top to provide a stop for the fall.

Record Holder

The whole thing is of $\frac{1}{4}$ in. plywood shaped as in Fig. 2. The main corners are through-dovetailed, and the intermediate divisions fit in shallow grooves.

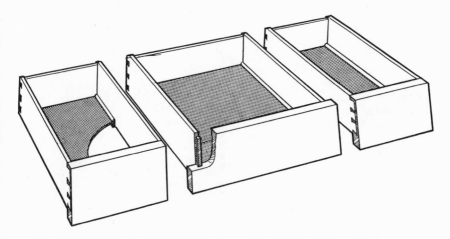

Fig. 4. CONSTRUCTION OF THE THREE DRAWERS

Stand

Fig. 3 shows the construction of this. The legs are bridle-jointed to the long rails, and are tapered from beneath the joints. The turned bottom ends can be either turned in the legs, or they can be turned separately and dowelled to the squares. Note that at the top the legs are square in section but are octagonal at the bottom. This effect is obtained by taper chamfering.

The long rails are joined by three cross rails slot-dovetailed in as in Fig. 3. Having fitted all joints the ends of the long rails are tapered, and the edges taper chamfered. To fix the stand to the carcase screws are driven through the rails. The holes are made a generous size to allow for possible movement. Alternatively, buttons could be used.

Finish the whole job with white or transparent french polish.

Cutting List

Carcase	Long ft.	in.	Wide in.	Thick in.
1 Top	3	$0\frac{1}{2}$	15	$\frac{3}{4}$
1 Shelf	3	0	$15\frac{1}{2}$	$\frac{3}{4}$
1 Bottom	3	0	$15\frac{1}{4}$	$\frac{3}{4}$
2 Ends	1	$9\frac{1}{4}$	$17\frac{1}{4}$	$\frac{3}{4}$
1 Back	3	0	21	$\frac{1}{4}$ ply
1 Slip	3	0	$1\frac{1}{2}$	$\frac{1}{4}$
2 Drawer fronts	0	$10\frac{1}{4}$	6	$\frac{3}{4}$
1 Drawer front	1	$3\frac{1}{2}$	6	$\frac{3}{4}$
6 Drawer sides	1	$3\frac{1}{2}$	5	$\frac{3}{8}$
2 Drawer backs	0	$10\frac{1}{4}$	$4\frac{1}{4}$	$\frac{3}{8}$
1 Drawer back	1	2	$4\frac{1}{4}$	$\frac{3}{8}$
2 Drawer bottoms..	0	10	15	$\frac{3}{16}$
1 Drawer bottom	1	$1\frac{1}{2}$	15	$\frac{3}{16}$
1 Fall panel	2	7	$10\frac{1}{4}$	$\frac{3}{4}$
2 Fall clamps	1	$2\frac{1}{2}$	$2\frac{1}{4}$	$\frac{3}{4}$
2 Fall rails	2	11	$2\frac{1}{4}$	$\frac{3}{4}$
Record Holder				
1 Top	2	11	$6\frac{1}{2}$	$\frac{1}{4}$
1 Bottom	2	11	$11\frac{1}{2}$	$\frac{1}{4}$
6 Uprights	1	$2\frac{1}{2}$	$11\frac{1}{2}$	$\frac{1}{4}$
1 Shelf	0	8	10	$\frac{1}{4}$
1 Shelf	0	8	8	$\frac{1}{4}$
Stand				
4 Legs (without separate feet)	1	0	—	$1\frac{3}{4}$ sq.
2 Rails	3	0	$2\frac{1}{2}$	$\frac{7}{8}$
3 Rails	1	2	$2\frac{1}{2}$	$1\frac{1}{4}$

Note that the uprights of the record holder can be cut economically, marking the top of one adjacent to the bottom of the other. Working allowance has been made in lengths and widths. Thicknesses are net.

Index